S

MW00586976

CROSS-CHECK

51767

CROSS-CHECK

*Integrating Building Systems
and Working Drawings*

Pat Guthrie

ROBESON COMMUNITY COLLEGE
LIBRARY
PO BOX 1420
LUMBERTON, NC 28359

McGraw-Hill

New York   San Francisco   Washington, D.C.   Auckland   Bogotá
Caracas   Lisbon   London   Madrid   Mexico City   Milan
Montreal   New Delhi   San Juan   Singapore
Sydney   Tokyo   Toronto

Library of Congress Cataloging-in-Publication Data

Guthrie, John Patten.
    Cross-check: integrating building systems and working drawings /
John Patten Guthrie.
        p.   cm.
    Includes index.
    ISBN 0-07-025304-8 (acid-free paper)
    1. Architecture—Designs and plans—Working drawings—Quality
control.   I. Title.
NA2713.G88   1998
720'.22'2—dc21   97-35381
                                                                CIP

McGraw-Hill

*A Division of The **McGraw·Hill** Companies*

Copyright © 1998 by The McGraw-Hill Companies, Inc. All rights reserved.
Printed in the United States of America. Except as permitted under the United
States Copyright Act of 1976, no part of this publication may be reproduced or dis-
tributed in any form or by any means, or stored in a data base or retrieval system,
without the prior written permission of the publisher.

1 2 3 4 5 6 7 8 9 0   DOC/DOC   9 0 2 1 0 9 8 7

ISBN 0-07-025304-8

*The sponsoring editor for this book was Wendy Lochner, the editing supervisor was
Bernard Onken, and the production supervisor was Tina Cameron. It was set in Janson
by North Market Street Graphics.*

Printed and bound by R. R. Donnelley & Sons Company.

McGraw-Hill books are available at special quantity discounts to use as premiums
and sales promotions, or for use in corporate training programs. For more information, please write to the Director of Special Sales, McGraw-Hill, 11 West 19th
Street, New York, NY 10011. Or contact your local bookstore.

Information contained in this work has been obtained by The McGraw-Hill
Companies, Inc. ("McGraw-Hill") from sources believed to be reliable. However, neither McGraw-Hill nor its authors guarantees the accuracy or completeness of any information published herein and neither McGraw-Hill nor its
authors shall be responsible for any errors, omissions, or damages arising out of
use of this information. This work is published with the understanding that
McGraw-Hill and its authors are supplying information but are not attempting
to render engineering or other professional services. If such services are
required, the assistance of an appropriate professional should be sought.

This book is printed on recycled, acid-free paper containing a
minimum of 50% recycled de-inked fiber.

Dedicated to Jan, Eric, and Erin.

Contents

How to Use This Book

This book is intended for architects and other design professionals (building designers, interior designers, engineers, etc.) who are responsible for the production of construction documents ("working drawings" and specifications) in designing buildings.

It is assumed that the user is familiar with the basics of making construction documents for building projects.

Cross-Check is a system for checking the coordination of working drawings. It can be used for any size project, from the smallest to the largest.

For the best use of this book, read it once and work the exercise in the last chapter. Then, continually use the Cross-Check system in Chapter 3 for all future projects. Freely add your own notes as your experience warrants.

Chapter 1

Checking and Back-Checking

THE BUILDING DESIGN PROCESS

Long ago, the American Institute of Architects (AIA) documented a five-phase logical sequence of the design and construction of buildings from the architect's perspective. The five phases are:

1. *Schematic Design (SD)*: Very early designing — 15%
2. *Design Development (DD)*: Full development of design — 20%
3. *Construction Documents (CD)*: Documentation of the design by working drawings and specs — 40%
4. *Bid/Negotiation (BN)*: Selecting a builder (and getting permits) — 5%
5. *Construction Administration (CA)*: Architect's observation during construction of the building — 20%

— 100%

As the process goes from one phase to the next, the design "hardens up" and becomes more detailed. The further along you are in the process, the harder (and more expensive) it is to backtrack and redesign due to error or a change of mind. It's like a big circle in the beginning that gets smaller and smaller as the process becomes more and more detailed. To jump backward from a ring to a larger ring is problematic. If one ever had to jump from the smallest ring back to the largest, it would be a disaster. In fact, one would be starting all over again, as if it were a whole new project. The idea is to be careful, so that you never have to backtrack.

The following sketch shows this concept and describes each phase in more detail:

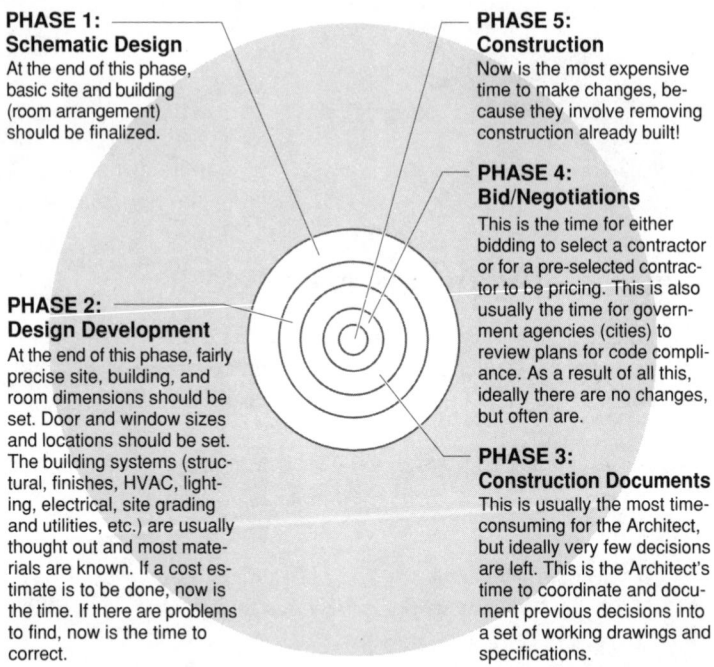

PHASE 1:
Schematic Design
At the end of this phase, basic site and building (room arrangement) should be finalized.

PHASE 2:
Design Development
At the end of this phase, fairly precise site, building, and room dimensions should be set. Door and window sizes and locations should be set. The building systems (structural, finishes, HVAC, lighting, electrical, site grading and utilities, etc.) are usually thought out and most materials are known. If a cost estimate is to be done, now is the time. If there are problems to find, now is the time to correct.

PHASE 5:
Construction
Now is the most expensive time to make changes, because they involve removing construction already built!

PHASE 4:
Bid/Negotiations
This is the time for either bidding to select a contractor or for a pre-selected contractor to be pricing. This is also usually the time for government agencies (cities) to review plans for code compliance. As a result of all this, ideally there are no changes, but often are.

PHASE 3:
Construction Documents
This is usually the most time-consuming for the Architect, but ideally very few decisions are left. This is the Architect's time to coordinate and document previous decisions into a set of working drawings and specifications.

THE CONSTRUCTION DOCUMENTS

Going back to the list of phases on page 1, the percentages on the right give approximations of the percentage of a total fee charged for each phase and thus reflects the amount of work, on average, each phase requires. The 40% attributed to the CD phase is the largest of any phase. Even for small projects, there is a lot of work in doing the technical "working drawings" and specifications. The Cross-Check system aids you in doing correct CDs.

THE DRAWINGS

The idea of drawings that show how the building is to be put together is very simple. The analogy of cutting a cake is helpful. Imagine that we have a layered cake that we are going to cut, put back together, and cut again.

THE PLANS

Cutting the cake horizontally, lifting off the top, and looking down represent the "plans" of the building because different types of plans "cut" the building as if the top is lifted off to reveal the layers below. The Foundation Plan represents a cut near the bottom of the cake. The Floor Plan cuts further up where the windows and doors are. The Reflected Ceiling Plan cuts just below the ceiling as if it is reflected in a mirror, below. The HVAC (heating, ventilation, and air conditioning) Plan cuts above the ceiling to show the duct layout. The Framing Plan cuts a little higher through the structural roof or floor framing. The Roof Plan just looks down on top. For very simple buildings, these few "cuts" might do. For more complex buildings, the Floor Plan has to be repeated a number of times to show different types of information, such as the Electrical Plan, which shows the switching and wiring.

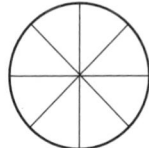 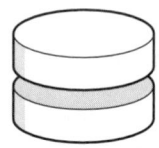

THE SECTIONS AND ELEVATIONS

Continuing the cake analogy, if the cake is cut vertically in two and you look at one side of the cut, it is like a building section which has been cut to reveal how it is built. A close look at where one layer meets another in the cake is like looking at a building detail. Finally, by putting the cake back together and looking from the side, it is like looking at the elevations of a building.

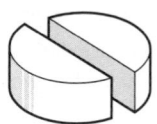 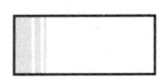

A SIMPLE IDEA, BUT HARD TO DO

Like viewing cake cuttings, drawing building plans is a simple concept. It is easy to understand how to cut the cake various ways to show what's inside. For the plans of a dog house, the cake analogy works. The problem is that for most modern buildings, even small, simple ones, no cake could ever be as intricate. This is particularly true for buildings in the United States, with increasingly more complex structural, mechanical, and electrical systems. So, the idea remains simple—cut the cake different ways, but the cake is getting ever more complex.

ERRORS

A set of drawings (CADD or hand-drawn) can look very good, but be totally miscoordinated and wrong. On the other hand, a sloppy-looking set of drawings can be well-coordinated and complete. Looks can be deceiving.

The drawings need to show the various layers of the building and section cuts, aligned, so that they all fit together. This sounds simple as pie (or to continue the analogy . . . cake). But, because the cake has become so complex, it gets ever harder to be sure all the pieces fit.

In theory, there should be no errors, because as each little decision is made and drawn, it will be thought out correctly. However, with the pressure of time and complexity involved, each little decision is not always thought out correctly. As an example, the architect locates a door where the engineer has put an electrical panel. This *conflict* in the drawings has to be found (the idea of this book) and then corrected (one or the other has to move to a new location).

Although errors are unavoidable, the architect (and design professionals) should strive to make as few as possible and then find and correct as many as possible. This book was written to aid in this process.

ARE ERRORS IN THE DOCUMENTS IMPORTANT?

There are some who believe that errors in the drawings and specifications, though undesirable, are not that important because they will all be worked out in the field anyway. Corollary thoughts are: (1) the drawings are not that important (they are only needed to get a building permit) because the contractor or owner will change everything, anyway; (2) the more detailed and bigger the CDs, the more the contractor charges. People who subscribe to these philosophies should probably not buy this book.

In theory, at least, it is true that it is not always necessary to have plans on paper to build a building. The plans can be in a person's head. Many buildings are built this way in other countries. But it's not a good idea and seldom can be done legally in the United States.

Some architects with forgiving contractors or rich clients may not need to worry about the quality of the plans. But this is really just being sloppy and unprofessional. Most architects will get into trouble with this approach. With the number of lawsuits growing in this country (even if often unwarranted), it pays for the architect and other design professionals to be diligent.

WHO IS RESPONSIBLE?

This book begins with the premise that one of the architect's jobs is to not only start the design process, but to wrap it up at the CD phase by checking to see that the CDs are complete and coordinated. There is no such thing as a perfect set of documents, but we can try.

The question is not who is responsible for errors, since anyone can make an error (but design professionals who are continually error-prone, with sloppy work, should probably go into another field). The question is, who will make the effort to find and correct errors?

Every design professional on the team should strive to avoid errors and back-check his or her own work. However, this book takes the position that it is the architect (or lead design professional responsible for the CDs) that is the one most responsible. Who else is going to do it? Who else is responsible for the big picture and overall coordination?

Engineers and other consultants usually have blinders on, doing their work as fast as they can to make a profit or meet a deadline. They don't necessarily think about the other people involved. If a consultant does consider the other aspects, treat that person like gold. Nevertheless, don't plan or rely on this type of consultant. Just as the general contractor's job is to coordinate the trades during construction, the architect's job is to coordinate the design and the documentation of the design . . . the drawings.

AVOIDING ERRORS

From the very beginning, the architect's job, as lead designer, is to check for errors, his or her own as well as those of others. This starts with the basic zoning of the property. The architect that develops a design without checking the legal allowable use by the local zoning law is like a surgeon that doesn't check which leg he or she is amputating. When this goes wrong, it's inexcusable!

The basics need to be taken care of during the SD phase. Zoning requirements should be checked to establish the building size and location on the property. The building's form and basic components and systems should be evolving. The building's cost should be roughly checked against the budget. This is the time to catch the big problems. Is the building too large or too tall, and are there enough parking spaces to comply with the local zoning ordinance? Is the style and form of the building too expensive for the client's budget? Checking for all these factors is critical in order for the most costly errors to be avoided. This phase is like laying a solid foundation on which to build.

The DD phase allows the design to progress in more detail. For small to medium-sized buildings, site/floor plan layouts at $1'' = 10''$ in the SD phase now grow to a much larger ¼" floor plan. The building code needs to be checked for compliance for occupancy, construction type, exiting, toilet room layout, etc. This is the time to finalize decisions on structural, mechanical, and electrical systems. If a full-cost estimate is to be done, this might be the best time to do it. At the end of this phase, the design work is finished and everyone is (hopefully) happy with the aesthetics (including any required design review boards by city governments). Ideally, the technical systems are worked out with enough detail so that enough space is allocated to the structural, mechanical, and electrical systems. In other words, the shell, framing, lighting, and the ductwork are all roughly coordinated, if not in final detail. Doing this coordination properly will avoid headaches down the road.

Ideally, very little design is left to be done in the CD phase. All that is left is documenting and working out previous decisions in detail.

TYPES OF WORKING DRAWING ERRORS

In the CD phase, the production of architectural and engineering working drawings is a very time-consuming and detailed process. Errors always creep into the process. Elimination of as many errors as possible is fundamental to a successful building project.

Errors can be of two kinds. First is the error of forgetting something which leaves an item out of the plans. Fred Stitt's series of checklists published under his *Guidelines* (as well as his *Working Drawing Manual*) are excellent tools for finding these types of errors.

Errors of miscoordination between the different types of disciplines, layers of information, and sheets of drawings are the second type. William Nigro's *Redicheck Interdisciplinary Coordination* booklet is an excellent (and the only one known to the author) tool for finding these types of errors.

The Cross-Check system is a more detailed way of doing coordination checking. It is a matrix system of checking drawing sheet against drawing sheet. The Cross-Check system will be introduced in Chapter 3.

Systematic checking and back-checking of the CDs is one of the hardest things the architect or lead design professional does. Toward the end of this phase, because so much time and effort has been already spent, the architect and other design professionals involved are usually tired of looking at the drawings and getting sick of the project. The stress of meeting a deadline also does not help.

Yet, this is exactly the time to put the effort into back-checking the drawings and specifications. This extra effort is not so much an intellectual exercise as an emotional one. Architects should make themselves do it as a commitment to excellence. Therefore, in the planning of the project, and the CD phase in particular, reserve time and emotional effort at the end for back-checking.

Probably the best way to back-check is to have someone (or a small team), completely independent of the project, do the back-check. Because of human nature, it is hard for professionals to find errors in their own work. It is easier (and more fun) to find errors in someone else's work. But it is not always practical to bring in a whole new person or team to do this. With the right attitude and commitment, the architect (or design professional) in charge can still do the back-check.

As mentioned before, there are a number of back-checks that should be done:

1. Back-check for completeness (were things forgotten?).
2. Back-check for legal compliance. The Uniform Building Code publishes a checklist. There are several checklists for compliance with the Americans with Disabilities Act.
3. Back-check for coordination of the CDs.

There is the story of the older architect turning over just-completed plans to his clients and saying: "Gentlemen, there is at least one error in these drawings. I have tried and tried to find it, but can't." A set of drawings with just one error or a few errors is very good. The point is, the drawings will probably never be perfect, but they can be close to it.

To conclude, the architect (or prime design professional) needs to always plan on back-checking in its various forms. The rest of this book deals with one type of back-checking—coordination.

Chapter 2

Coordination

WHY IT'S HARD

Back-checking for coordination of the working drawings and specifications is probably the hardest type of back-check to do. It seems reasonable that a few little things are forgotten or a few little unforeseen
technical code problems come up. But as the CDs were produced, it
was necessary to do coordination. So, it may not seem reasonable to
have to back-check for coordination. But it should be done, because
despite the best efforts, miscoordination can happen.

COORDINATE AS YOU GO

To minimize coordination problems, start coordinating from the very
beginning.

Planning at the beginning of working drawings can be very important for proper coordination of drawings. As an example, take time
to think through and plan for naming and numbering all rooms, as
this information may be repeated by consultants. Setting up the column locations with their grid designations is something else that will
be repeated. Any change in these basic elements will require making
similar changes throughout the set of drawings, which could result in
errors. The point is, take time to do these basics right in the first
place, so they won't have to be changed later. A list of basics:

1. Sheet names and numbers
2. Column grid locations and designations
3. Wall locations
4. Room name and numbers

A handy technique is to denote on each detail the sheet number or detail number where this particular detail is "cut." This gives the user of the drawings valuable information, but also forces coordination of the details.

Be specific in the plans. "See Detail 5/S-2" is better than "see the structural drawings."

Duplication of information is always a problem. For instance, structural notes versus specifications. The specifications repeat most of the information the engineer wants in the structural notes on the drawings. Doing this repeats the same information, which is an opening for miscoordination. As an example, the engineer changes something on the structural notes, so they say one thing and the specifications say another. To avoid this kind of inconsistency, eliminate one or the other, or have one refer to the other.

Drawings often refer to one another. In a pinch and to be safe:

1. Have HVAC and Electrical Lighting plans refer to the architectural Reflected Ceiling Plan for exact locations of ceiling diffusers and lights.
2. Have Structural Plans refer to mechanical plans for coordination of exact location of roof- or floor-mounted equipment, and vice versa.

Look for engineering (or other consultant) changes that unknowingly cause inconsistencies in other things. Be sure all consultants and other team members notify the architect (and/or other team members) whenever they make a change.

Specifications are often not taken seriously by contractors, because they are often "canned." That is, they have standard verbiage that often does not apply to the project. The specifications should be as brief as possible and be directly pertinent to the project. Although detailed coordination between the Specifications and the Drawings is not the major subject of this book, mention should be made that one way to begin to coordinate is to simply review all the sections of the Construction Specifications Institute (CSI) format to see what applies to the project. At the end of the CD phase, review the specifications to see that everything included reflects what is in the drawings. If not, it usually should be taken out of the specifications. To aid in this process, see Appendix A, which shows the latest CSI format.

Everyone involved with the project should look for errors. A draftsperson that questions things that do not seem right is worth gold.

BACK-CHECKING COORDINATION

It is best to back-check documents prior to publication (for large projects, do back-checks periodically, at 25, 50, and 75% of completion). If the time pressure is just too great, do it prior to permitting, and in the worst case, do it while bidding.

Deciding how far to check, especially in the engineering specialties, is always a problem. Checking that parapet signs have power to them is reasonable. But checking if the signs are powered correctly is usually beyond the architect's expertise.

A consultant can usually be relied on to fix problems when found. But you cannot rely on the consultant to find the problem in the first place. Sometimes just asking "Did you check this, did you remember that?" will remind the consultant of what he or she might have forgotten. But you have to remember to ask in the first place.

At the beginning, the back-checker should quickly glance over each sheet of the set of drawings to become familiar with the overall project. One way to do a fast cross-check is to have each discipline present.

Planning: For the typical project of average complexity, plan on approximately 45 minutes per sheet for checking. For simple projects with small sheets, allow 30 minutes per sheet. For complex projects with large sheets, allow 1 hour per sheet.

Use prints, not originals, for back-checking.

Provide room to lay out print sheets. Use of a light table to lay one print over another is excellent. Use a window in a pinch.

Use of different-color markers is helpful. For instance, color all lights yellow when overlaying electrical lighting to Reflected Ceiling Plan and color all ceiling diffusers and return air grilles blue when overlaying HVAC Plans to the Reflected Ceiling Plan.

"Registration" is often a problem. Ideally, every plan should be in perfect registration, but this seldom happens due to the "stretch" of the printing process. Even computer plots are sometimes a problem.

In back-checking for coordination, usually the best thing to do is to just find the problem first and solve it later. Don't try to solve it then and there.

The next chapter will provide the system that can help you with coordination checking.

Chapter 3

Cross-Check

On page 23 you will find the Cross-Check Matrix for a hypothetical set of working drawings for what appears to be a small but complex project. It appears small because the architectural and structural plans are not separated. It appears complex because it includes demolition (implying a remodel project), interior design, and special equipment. The detail sheets are not included in the matrix.

Actually, it is a generic matrix and checklist system that can be used for just about any project. If your project does not have a second story (and has a slab-on-grade floor that is shown on the Foundation Plan), then disregard the Floor Framing Plan. If the project is a 10-story building, then the Floor Plan, Floor Framing Plan, HVAC Plan, Plumbing Plan, and Electrical Plan apply 10 times (or for each story). If there is no remodeling, disregard the demolition plans (Demo Site Plan and Demo Plan). Many remodeling projects may not have these specific plans because the information they provide is on the "normal" sheets. Nevertheless, the checklist items would still apply. If interior design is not involved, then disregard the Decor-Furniture Plan. If the project has no special equipment (as, say, for a factory) then disregard the Special Equipment, Schedules, and Rough-in Plans.

This generic list of drawings should cover most projects in general, if not in detail. Pages 17 through 20 give a brief description of what each generic drawing might include.

Past the matrix, from pages 25 through 93, is the Cross-Check Checklist. On the right side is the checklist and a brief discussion of each checklist item is on the left.

Going back to the matrix on page 23, the same generic list of drawings goes down the page and across the page. A grid is created with an intersection box for each drawing in relation to another. You will notice that every box is numbered (1 through 408). Each box is a potential place for checking one drawing against another.

The same numbers are used again in the checklist. As an example, on page 23 in the matrix, find the box for checking the Floor Plan against the Floor Framing Plan. This is item 202. Now, go to page 59 and you will see item 202 with the checklist item:

202. FLOOR PLAN / FLOOR FRAME

A. Exterior wall locations

B. Column locations

C. Interior bearing walls

D. Floor openings

E. Window locations for headers

To the left, on page 58, you will see an explanation of the checklist:

202. FLOOR PLAN TO FLOOR FRAMING PLAN:

Items shown on the Floor Plan that are structural or require structural framing, should match on both plans. Such items are exterior wall locations, column size and locations, interior bearing wall locations, floor openings and widow (and sometimes, door) width and locations (for structural headers or lintels).

The purpose of having the checklist in simple format and the explanation in a more narrative format is to remind the architect to check the Floor Plan against the Roof Framing Plan for the same wall and column locations, and anything that goes from the floor up through the roof, like a ladder or set of stairs.

Going back to the matrix, you will see that some boxes are shaded and some are white. The shaded boxes indicate a generic checklist item. These are items that a typical project would have. The boxes left white have none, indicating there would typically be nothing to check. However, a "real" project might have some unusual conditions. As an example, a building design has landscape planter boxes under each exterior window, which is not a typical situation. The Landscape Plan would show the material in the box and the Irrigation Plan might show a drip system. Since the boxes are built-in construction, they are likely to be shown on the Floor Plan, Building Sections, Elevations, and Wall Sections. This might involve items 133, 135, 139, 143, and 146, to check that these drawings show the planters at the same place and the same size.

A particular architect's office may have work in certain building types, or any other particular circumstances that require new checklist items. As an example, for restaurants, the Interior Elevations should always show the cooking hood indicated on the Special Equipment Plan. So, #360 would be shaded, and on page 85 in the checklist at #360 write in:

360. INTERIOR ELEV / SPEC EQUIP PL
B. Show cook hoods

and if desired, on the left side (page 84), add:

360. INTERIOR ELEVATIONS TO SPECIAL EQUIPMENT PLANS:
Always show cooking hoods on interior elevations.

Items should be filled in as the architect sees fit, but care should be taken. The Cross-Check system does not include checking each and every sheet against another for continuity of the plan (wall and grid locations) or such things as north arrows. If this is added, probably every box will be shaded and the system will get cluttered. Rather, it is best to realize that *it is understood* that each drawing must be checked for this type of continuity.

The Cross-Check system can be used in several ways:

- First, using the "blanks" on pages 21 and 22; a matrix and checklist can be created. This might be done for very complex projects, but this can be very time consuming and get overly complex.

- Second, use the generic list of plans, as given, and write in beside each drawing the sheet numbers that apply. Then, outline in red each box that applies.

- Third, and the fastest way, is to simply and quickly go down the checklist and check for items that apply to the project.

However the Cross-Check system is used, if time permits, some sort of "check-off" method should be used to ascertain everything has been found. This could be by "X"ing in each box, shading each box red, or putting a check next to each applicable item in the checklist when done.

It is not suggested that the checklist system be used, only to point out coordination problems. It is best to "redline" a set of check prints. As an example, in checking Floor Plan A101 against Structural Plan S103, it is apparent that column G-5 is not shown at the same location between the two corresponding sheets. A redline should be done at the column location on Drawing A101 . . . "Location conflicts with Drawing S103," and on Drawing S103 a redline would be made . . . "Location conflicts with Drawing A101." *If it is clear* which sheet is wrong, only that sheet would have to be redlined.

In coordination checking, as in all types of checking, it is usually better to find all errors before working on the solutions. Do not mindlessly use the Cross-Check system. Think through every step. The system cannot possibly think of every point of coordination on a real project.

When using the checklist, one item might bring to mind something else to check. Either go ahead and check it, or write it down for later checking. Do not lose the thought.

The Cross-Check system does not check for technically correct design, but only for coordination of items. As an example, it does not check the size of a beam, but checks that a beam and some other item (such as a duct) are not in the same place. Another example would be that the cross-check is intended to check that each light fixture on the Reflected Ceiling Plan is also on the Electrical Lighting Plan (and in the same location), not to check the electrical design of the lighting plan (wiring size, etc.).

The Cross-Check system can be used by the architect (or the prime design professional) or the architect can give disciplines sections appropriate to them for checking.

The architect might feel that checking the mechanical, plumbing, and electrical (MPE) items (as well as the special equipment items) are above and beyond the call of duty. In that case the MPE consultants should cross-check their own drawings.

The Cross-Check system can also be used when the client wants to make changes to the design in the middle of the CD phase. As mentioned in Chapter 1, this is not the time to do this. When all is going well, very small changes will naturally occur during the CD phase due to small inconsistencies that come to light or detailed decisions not previously made. Thus small changes do not hurt, though they should not be encouraged. The problem is in the big changes, such as rearrangement of rooms. The client often doesn't differentiate between small and big changes. When a big change occurs, the Cross-Check system can be used for two purposes.

First, to define the scope of work for the change, the matrix can be used to identify what drawings will have to be revised. If the change proceeds, use the system to do it correctly. Changes, for whatever reason, during the CD phase, are going to be a major source of errors, because they are often made in haste to meet a deadline and often everyone involved is tired.

Second, a major change usually involves a renegotiation of fee and time schedule. The client is often shocked at the extra fees and time lost. He or she does not appreciate the degree of intricacy involved in a set of construction documents and how changes on one drawing can affect a number of other drawings. By showing the client the marked-up matrix, it will provide a visual idea of the work involved. This will hopefully convince him or her that the change is not worth it or that extra money and lost time are needed to make the change.

EXPLANATION OF CROSS-CHECK GENERIC PLANS

- SURVEY: Usually provided by others, showing site boundaries, existing surface objects, land contours or spot elevations, and utilities both above and underground. In the case of the remodel of an existing building, the "survey" might mean "existing conditions" plans. The idea is to show what one has to start with . . . the physical restraints of the project.

- SITE PLAN: This plan shows the proposed building (or buildings) laid out on the site, with all site objects (parking, curbs, sidewalks, etc.) in their relationship to the building. One of the most important functions of this plan is to horizontally dimension the building and objects to the property lines.

- DEMOLITION SITE PLAN: In the case where site "remodeling" occurs, this plan documents what site objects stay and what is removed.

- GRADING AND DRAINAGE PLAN: This special site plan shows the vertical "alignment" of the site for proper drainage. By contours or by spot elevations, or both, all surface objects, including the building floor slab, are assigned vertical elevations in relation to some datum point.

- SITE UTILITY PLAN: This special site plan may be one sheet (highly preferable for coordination). More likely, this represents a composite of: the civil engineer's water, sewer, and storm drain (if not on the grading and drainage plan); the electrical engineer's power and telephone plan (as well as site and landscape lighting); and, the mechanical engineer's gas plan. It represents all the utilities brought to the building.

- LANDSCAPE PLAN: This special site plan shows all landscaping being added to the site. It might also show existing landscaping to be removed or to remain.

- IRRIGATION PLAN: This plan shows all watering systems for landscaping (flood, spray, or drip).

- FOUNDATION PLAN: This plan shows the footings or foundation system to support the superstructure of the building. Systems can be spread footings, spot footings, drilled piers, or piles. Each column and bearing wall should be denoted and located with its foundation shown. Also, any change of elevation of a slab on grade should be shown.

- FLOOR PLAN: This plan (or plans) is usually the "heart" of the set of drawings, as it shows the overall layout of each floor of the building. All walls are located and all rooms identified (as well as all doors and windows).

- DEMOLITION FLOOR PLAN: In the case of remodel and addition projects, this plan (or plans) denotes plans of existing buildings, where existing items are to be saved or removed. In a very complex project, this concept might extend to demolition foundation, structural frame, reflected ceiling plans etc.

- DECOR-FURNITURE PLAN: This represents any plans showing decor objects and, particularly, furniture layout. Although the general contractor often will not be concerned with these plans, since they will not be his or her responsibility, they are why all the other plans are done . . . to produce a livable and workable building. Often these are done by others, in a different set of drawings.

- REFLECTED CEILING PLAN: This represents the ceiling plan for each floor of the building. It calls out the height and materials of each ceiling in each room and shows all objects that touch or penetrate the ceiling (lights, walls, diffusers, etc.).

- FLOOR FRAMING PLAN: This represents all structural plans showing the framing of each floor level. The floor is shown with its under support of joists, purlins, beams, and girders. Bearing walls are also shown. Any special heavy equipment sitting on the floor (or suspended, below) is framed. Openings such as stairs, elevators, and duct shafts are also framed.

- ROOF FRAMING PLAN: As the floor framing plan/s frame the floor(s), this does the same for the roof. Small- to medium-size buildings are often loaded with roof-mounted AC equipment, so this plan must show framing for their supports and openings.

- ROOF PLAN: This plan shows the drainage pattern of the roof and locates all roof-mounted equipment and other objects and openings. In the Cross-Check system, it is assumed that spot elevations are denoted on this plan, although they could be on the roof framing plan.

- SCHEDULES: This denotes sheets showing architectural schedules such as the Room Finish Schedule, Door Schedule, and Window Schedule.

- BUILDING SECTIONS: This sheet(s) vertically cuts through the building at certain strategic locations to show its overall construction. The Floor Plan(s) and Building Sections do more to quickly explain the building than any other sheets.

- ELEVATIONS: The exterior sides of the building are shown on this sheet(s).

- INTERIOR ELEVATIONS: The wall surface areas of all of the rooms are shown on these sheets.

- WALL SECTIONS: This sheet(s) cuts through the various types of wall assemblies to show them in detail. Any structural elements for floors and roof framed into the wall are shown.

- MECHANICAL, PLUMBING, AND ELECTRICAL ROOF PLAN: This plan represents the mechanical and electrical engineers' drawings dealing with roof-mounted equipment, when this occurs. It might actually be three sheets (HVAC, plumbing, and electrical) at different locations in the set of drawings. If mechanical equipment is located in a room or rooms, this may represent a check of these. If there is roof-mounted equipment, but no MPE

Roof Plan, check to see that the equivalent information is on the HVAC, plumbing, and/or electrical plans.

- HVAC PLANS: This represents the mechanical engineer's plans for heating, ventilation, and air conditioning of each floor of the building.

- PLUMBING PLANS: This represents the mechanical engineer's plans for "plumbing" of the building's water and waste systems. Gas is usually included here, when used.

- ELECTRICAL POWER PLANS: This represents the electrical engineer's plans for "powering" of the building. All power requiring objects are properly accounted for and tied into the electrical system. Included are exit and emergency lighting (if not shown on the lighting plan).

- ELECTRICAL LIGHTING PLANS: This is the plan(s) that shows all electric lighting and how it is tied into the building's power system. Sometimes the lighting is also shown on a special sheet by the lighting consultant.

- SPECIAL EQUIPMENT PLANS: This represents various types of equipment that the building houses. It might be factory equipment, supermarket coolers and casework, dental equipment, or kitchen equipment for a restaurant. In any case, when used, this equipment must be allocated space and sometimes must be wired, plumbed, or ventilated. Sometimes it must have special floor conditions, concrete curbs, or depressions.

- SPECIAL EQUIPMENT SCHEDULES: When any special equipment is extensive, the designers of the equipment layout will often provide a schedule showing each piece of equipment's needs (water, waste, power, gas, etc.).

- SPECIAL EQUIPMENT ROUGH-INS: When the special equipment is extensive, sometimes the equipment consultants will provide "rough-in" plans locating each piece of equipment on the floorplan and locating (horizontally and vertically) the utility connections and sizes (water, waste, power, gas, etc.).

CROSS-CHECK MATRIX

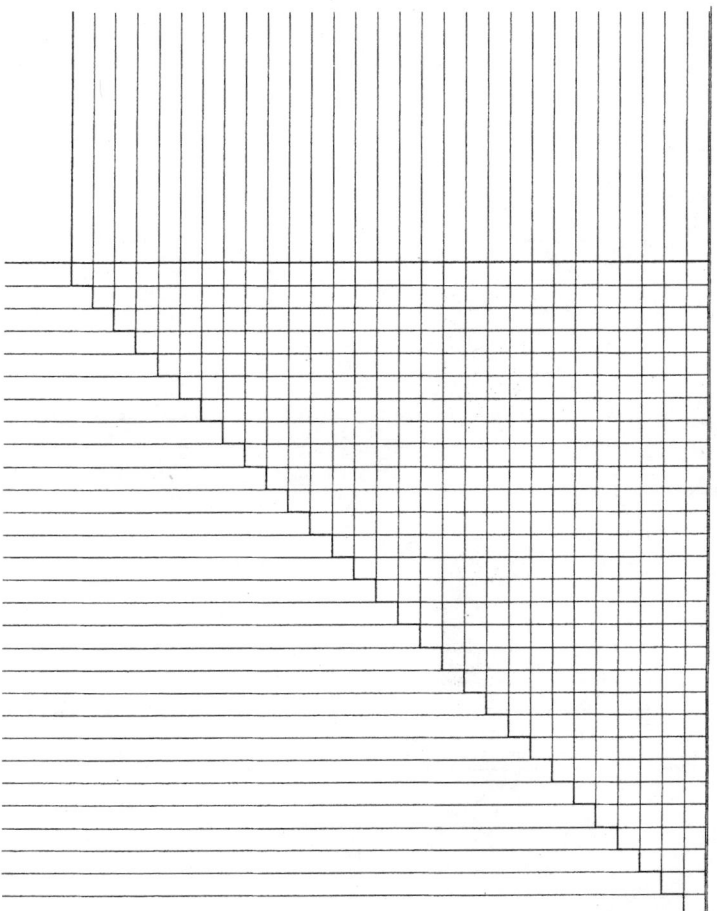

CROSS-CHECK

CROSS-CHECK MATRIX

	SURVEY	SITE PLAN	DEMO SITE PL	GRAD'G & DRAIN.	SITE UTILITY PLAN	LANDSCAPE PLAN	IRRIGATION PLAN	FOUNDATION PLAN	FLOOR PLAN/S	DEMO FLOOR PLAN/S	DECOR/FURNITURE PLAN/S	REFLECTED CEILING PLAN/S	FLOOR FRAMING PLAN/S	ROOF FRAMING PLAN	ROOF PLAN	SCHEDULES	BUILDING SECTIONS	ELEVATIONS	INTERIOR ELEVATIONS	WALL SECTIONS	M.P.E. ROOF PLAN	H.V.A.C. PLAN/S	PLUMBING PLAN/S	ELECTRICAL POWER PLAN/S	ELECTRICAL LIGHTING PLAN/S	SPECIAL EQUIPMENT PLAN/S	SPECIAL EQUIPMENT SCHEDULE/S	SPECIAL EQUIPMENT ROUGH-INS
SURVEY	1	2	3	4	5	6	7	8	9	10	11	12	13	14	15	16	17	18	19	20	21	22	23	24	25	26	27	28
SITE PLAN		29	30	31	32	33	34	35	36	37	38	39	40	41	42	43	44	45	46	47	48	49	50	51	52	53	54	55
DEMO SITE PL			56	57	58	59	60	61	62	63	64	65	66	67	68	69	70	71	72	73	74	75	76	77	78	79	80	81
GRAD'G & DRAIN.			82	83	84	85	86	87	88	89	90	91	92	93	94	95	96	97	98	99	100	101	102	103	104	105	106	107
SITE UTILITY PLAN					108	109	110	111	112	113	114	115	116	117	118	119	120	121	122	123	124	125	126	127	128	129	130	131
LANDSCAPE PLAN						132	133	134	135	136	137	138	139	140	141	142	143	144	145	146	147	148	149	150	151	152	153	154
IRRIGATION PLAN							155	156	157	158	159	160	161	162	163	164	165	166	167	168	169	170	171	172	173	174	175	176
FOUNDATION PLAN								177	178	179	180	181	182	183	184	185	186	187	188	189	190	191	192	193	194	195	196	197
FLOOR PLAN/S									198	199	200	201	202	203	204	205	206	207	208	209	210	211	212	213	214	215	216	217
DEMO FLOOR PLAN/S										218	219	220	221	222	223	224	225	226	227	228	229	230	231	232	233	234	235	236
DECOR / FURNITURE PLAN/S											237	238	239	240	241	242	243	244	245	246	247	248	249	250	251	252	253	254
REFLECTED CEILING PLAN/S												255	256	257	258	259	260	261	262	263	264	265	266	267	268	269	270	271
FLOOR FRAMING PLAN/S													272	273	274	275	276	277	278	279	280	281	282	283	284	285	286	287
ROOF FRAMING PLAN														288	289	290	291	292	293	294	295	296	297	298	299	300	301	302
ROOF PLAN															303	304	305	306	307	308	309	310	311	312	313	314	315	316
SCHEDULES																317	318	319	320	321	322	323	324	325	326	327	328	329
BUILDING SECTIONS																	330	331	332	333	334	335	336	337	338	339	340	341
ELEVATIONS																		342	343	344	345	346	347	348	349	350	351	352
INTERIOR ELEVATIONS																			353	354	355	356	357	358	359	360	361	362
WALL SECTIONS																				363	364	365	366	367	368	369	370	371
M.P.E. ROOF PLAN																					372	373	374	375	376	377	378	379
H.V.A.C. PLAN/S																						380	381	382	383	384	385	386
PLUMBING PLAN/S																							387	388	389	390	391	392
ELECTRICAL POWER PLAN/S																								393	394	395	396	397
ELECTRICAL LIGHTING PLAN/S																									398	399	400	401
SPECIAL EQUIPMENT PLAN/S																									402	403	404	405
SPECIAL EQUIPMENT SCHEDULE/S																											406	407
SPECIAL EQUIPMENT ROUGH-INS																												408

Cross-Check Checklist

2. SURVEY TO THE SITE PLAN:
Verify that property lines (length and bearing) are the same on each sheet. Verify any required setbacks and easements.

3. SURVEY TO DEMOLITION SITE PLAN:
Verify that all existing items shown on the survey are accounted for on the Demolition Site Plan and each item is denoted to remain or be removed.

4. SURVEY TO GRADING AND DRAINAGE PLAN:
Verify that the existing grades shown on the Survey are accounted for on the Grading and Drainage Plan, no matter how they are modified.

5. SURVEY TO SITE UTILITY PLAN:
Verify that the new are connected to the existing utilities where shown on the Survey. This would include water, sewer, power, telephone, gas, and storm drains, when applicable, as well as meters and vaults.

6. SURVEY TO LANDSCAPE PLAN:
Verify any existing landscape is accounted for on the new Landscape Plan.

7. SURVEY TO IRRIGATION PLAN:
Verify any existing irrigation is accounted for on the new Irrigation Plan. This might be by showing it or more likely, a note ("tie into existing irrigation system").

1. _____
_____
_____
_____
_____
_____

2. SURVEY/SITE PLAN
A. Boundary and property lines
B. Easements
_____
_____
_____

3. SURVEY/DEMO SITE PLAN
A. Existing to be removed
B. Existing to remain
_____
_____
_____

4. SURVEY/GRADING & DRAINAGE
A. Existing grades
_____
_____
_____

5. SURVEY/SITE UTILITY PLAN
A. Existing water
B. Existing sewer
C. Existing power
D. Existing telephone
E. Existing gas
F. Existing storm drains

6. SURVEY/LANDSCAPE PLAN
A. Existing landscape
_____
_____
_____

7. SURVEY/IRRIGATION PLAN
A. Existing irrigation
_____
_____
_____
_____

8. _____
_____
_____
_____
_____
_____

9. _____
_____
_____
_____
_____
_____

10. _____
_____
_____
_____
_____

11. _____
_____
_____
_____
_____
_____

12. _____
_____
_____
_____
_____

17. **SURVEY TO BUILDING SECTIONS:**

    At sites with steep slopes, the existing grades are often shown at the point where the building section is cut. This shows if the footings are in existing soils or in new fill.

18. **SURVEY TO ELEVATIONS:**

    At sites with steep slopes, existing grades are often dashed below the elevation, roughly indicating their location at the exterior wall.

12. _____
_____
_____
_____
_____
_____

13. _____
_____
_____
_____
_____
_____

14. _____
_____
_____
_____
_____
_____

15. _____
_____
_____
_____
_____
_____

16. _____
_____
_____
_____
_____
_____

17. SURVEY/BUILDING SECT.
A. Show exist'g grades at build'g
   sects _____
_____
_____
_____

18. SURVEY/ELEVATIONS
A. Show existing grades _____
_____
_____
_____
_____
_____

19. _____
_____
_____
_____
_____
_____

20. _____
_____
_____
_____
_____
_____

21. _____
_____
_____
_____
_____
_____

22. _____
_____
_____
_____
_____
_____

23. _____
_____
_____
_____
_____
_____

30. **SITE PLAN TO DEMOLITION SITE PLAN:**
    Verify that any existing items shown on the Demolition Site Plan that are to remain or to be removed, are accounted for on the new Site Plan.

31. **SITE PLAN TO GRADING AND DRAINAGE PLAN:**
    Verify that any built in changes of elevation such as steps and ramps shown on the Site Plan coordinate with the top and bottom grades shown on the Grading and Drainage Plan.

32. **SITE PLAN TO UTILITY SITE PLAN:**
    Verify that the Site Plan shows constructed objects that serve the utilities shown on the Utility Site Plan. These might be transformers, meters, power or telephone poles, etc.

33. **SITE PLAN TO LANDSCAPE PLAN:**
    Verify that objects shown on the Site Plan do not interfere with landscaping. These might be fire hydrants, meters, and signs that might be shown where trees are. Also trees might be located that interfere with the visibility of building signs. Verify that any constructed landscape boundaries, such as curbs, are shown on the Site Plan.

34. **SITE PLAN TO IRRIGATION PLAN:**
    To get from one landscape area to another, the irrigation piping must be sleeved under hard surfaces, such as walks. Verify that objects and areas that must be sleeved under are located the same on both plans.

35. **SITE PLAN TO FOUNDATION PLAN:**
    The site plan usually outlines the outer face of the first-floor stem wall, a definite point to dimension to. Verify that the outline of building is same for both plans.

24. _____
_____
_____
_____
_____
_____
_____

25. _____
_____
_____
_____
_____
_____
_____

26. _____
_____
_____
_____
_____
_____
_____

27. _____
_____
_____
_____
_____
_____
_____

28. _____
_____
_____
_____
_____
_____
_____

29. _____
_____
_____
_____
_____
_____

30. SITE/DEMO SITE PLAN
A. Site items to remain or be removed
_____
_____
_____
_____

31. SITE/GRADING & DRAINAGE
A. Steps
B. Ramps
_____
_____
_____

32. SITE/UTILITY SITE PLAN
A. Transformer pad
B. Power vaults
C. Meters
D. Manholes
E. Grease traps

33. SITE/LANDSCAPE PLAN
A. Landscape boundaries (curbs)
B. Objects in landscape areas (signs, light poles, etc.)
_____
_____

34. SITE/IRRIGATION PLAN
A. Sleeve irrigation under paving between landscape areas
_____
_____
_____

35. SITE/FOUNDATION PLAN
A. Building footprint
_____
_____
_____
_____

4   DISCUSSIONS

36. SITE PLAN TO FLOOR PLAN:
Verify that outline and overall dimensions of building are the same on both plans.

38. SITE PLAN TO DECOR/FURNITURE PLAN:
Where exterior furniture is used (patio tables and chairs, or benches, etc.), one plan may need to refer to the other to account for these.

42. SITE PLAN TO ROOF PLAN:
If roof drainage is external by downspouts or scuppers, splash blocks are often provided. These, shown on the Site Plan, should be in the same locations as the drainage outlets shown on the Roof Plan.

36. SITE/FLOOR PLAN
A. Building footprint
_____
_____
_____
_____

37. _____
_____
_____
_____
_____

38. SITE/DECOR-FURNITURE
A. Exterior furniture
_____
_____
_____
_____

39. _____
_____
_____
_____
_____

40. _____
_____
_____
_____
_____

41. _____
_____
_____
_____
_____

42. SITE PLAN/ROOF PLAN
A. Splash blocks from roof drainage
_____
_____
_____
_____

43. _____
_____
_____
_____
_____
_____

44. _____
_____
_____
_____
_____
_____

45. _____
_____
_____
_____
_____

46. _____
_____
_____
_____
_____

47. _____
_____
_____
_____
_____
_____

58. SITE DEMOLITION PLAN TO SITE UTILITY PLAN:
Where remodeling of an existing built site is required, there needs to be an accounting and coordination of existing utilities, whether they are to be removed, abandoned, or reused.

59. SITE DEMOLITION PLAN TO LANDSCAPE PLAN:
Verify that existing landscape materials shown on the Site Demolition plan are accounted for on the new Landscape Plan (removed, saved, etc.).

48. _____
_____
_____
_____
_____
_____

49. _____
_____
_____
_____
_____
_____

50. _____
_____
_____
_____
_____
_____

51. _____
_____
_____
_____
_____
_____

52. _____
_____
_____
_____
_____
_____

53. _____
_____
_____
_____
_____
_____

54. _____
_____
_____
_____
_____
_____

55. _____
_____
_____
_____
_____
_____

56. _____
_____
_____
_____
_____
_____

57. _____
_____
_____
_____
_____
_____

58. **SITE DEMO/SITE UTILITY**
A. Existing utilities to be removed
or saved (Water, Sewer, Power,
Gas, Tele., Storm sewer)
_____
_____

59. **SITE DEMO/LANDSCAPE**
A. Existing landscape to be
removed or saved
_____
_____
_____

60. SITE DEMOLITION PLAN TO IRRIGATION PLAN:

Verify that existing landscape irrigation shown on the Site Demolition Plan is accounted for on the new Irrigation Plan (removed, abandoned, or saved) etc.

61. SITE DEMOLITION PLAN TO FOUNDATION PLAN:

Where remodeling is required on an existing built-up site, there may be constructed objects that interfere with the new foundations. Existing foundations may have to be removed or tied into.

62. SITE DEMOLITION PLAN TO FLOOR PLAN:

Where remodeling is required on the site, there may be existing objects at the periphery of the building that interfere with new construction. How this is handled needs to be coordinated and explained on these plans.

63. SITE DEMOLITION PLAN TO DEMOLITION FLOOR PLAN:

At the peripheries of buildings, there are often objects that need to be shown on both site and floor plans. In the case of site remodeling, any such objects need to be shown and accounted for (saved, modified, or removed).

60. SITE DEMO/IRRIGATION

A. Existing irrigation to be
removed or saved

_____

_____

_____

61. SITE DEMO/FOUNDATION

A. Existing foundations to be
saved or removed

_____

_____

_____

62. SITE DEMO/FLOOR PLAN

A. Existing construction, next to
building, to be removed or
saved

_____

_____

63. SITE DEMO/DEMO FL PLAN

A. Existing construction to be
saved or removed (that would
show on both plans)

_____

_____

64. _____

_____

_____

_____

_____

65. _____

_____

_____

_____

_____

66. _____

_____

_____

_____

_____

_____

_____

67. _____

_____

_____

_____

_____

_____

68. _____

_____

_____

_____

_____

_____

69. _____

_____

_____

_____

_____

_____

70. _____

_____

_____

_____

_____

_____

71. _____

_____

_____

_____

_____

_____

83. GRADING AND DRAINAGE PLAN TO SITE UTILITY PLAN:
Where the site is to be drained by an underground storm system, verify that grading is coordinated with the underground system. (Often the storm drain system is shown on the Grading and Drainage Plan.)

72. _____

73. _____

74. _____

75. _____

76. _____

77. _____

78. _____

79. _____

80. _____

81. _____

82. _____

83. **GRAD'G & DRAIN/SITE UTILITY**
    A. Storm drains

84. GRADING AND DRAINAGE PLAN TO LANDSCAPE PLAN:

Verify that where drainage and ground slopes affect landscaping, the two are coordinated. Drainage swales, splash blocks, retention basins, and side slopes are the type of thing that might affect landscaping. Verify that the landscape material is compatible with conditions of slope or being in water. For instance, a slope may be so steep that the only material suitable would be rock. Where the landscape design introduces features like berms and embankments at the periphery or near the building, care should be taken that proper drainage away from the building is maintained, as called for on the Grading & Drainage Plan.

86. GRADING AND DRAINAGE PLAN TO FOUNDATION PLAN:

Verify that the depth of the foundations are coordinated with the grading. Steep grades along a building would require stepped footings.

87. GRADING AND DRAINAGE PLAN TO FLOOR PLAN:

Verify that the exterior door steps, landings, ramps, etc., are coordinated between the two drawings. Any of these types of items added to one plan for grade change need to be addressed on the other plan. For example, steps shown on the Floor Plan, need to be shown on the Grading & Drainage Plan, with spot elevations at top and bottom.

93. GRADING AND DRAINAGE PLAN TO ROOF PLAN:

Where the roof drainage somehow releases to the site (not a city storm drain system), verify that both plans are coordinated to show the same location and number of release points. This might be downspouts at the periphery of the building or underground pipes to a curb line. The drainage pattern needs to flow away from the building.

95. GRADING AND DRAINAGE PLAN TO BUILDING SECTIONS:

On each building section show the proper grades at the periphery of the building as determined by the grading plan. Building sections should show unusual grading conditions like basements or embankments at exterior retention walls.

84. GRAD'G. & DRAIN./LANDSCAPE
A. Swales w/ground covers
B. Retention basins w/ground covers
C. Slopes w/ground covers
D. Maintain proper grading away from building

85. _____

86. GRAD'G. & DRAIN./FOUND.
A. Depth of foundations

87. GRAD'G. & DRAIN./FLOOR PLAN
A. Steps & landings around the periphery of building

88. _____

89. _____

90. _____

91. _____

92. _____

93. GRAD'G. & DRAIN./ROOF
A. Roof drainage to site

94. _____

95. GRAD'G. & DRAIN./BLD'G. SECT.
A. Grades at periphery of building

96. GRADING AND DRAINAGE PLAN TO ELEVATIONS:
Verify that grades are coordinated on both sheets. Ideally, the elevations should show the grades at the periphery of the building, reflecting that shown on the Grading and Drainage Plan.

98. GRADING AND DRAINAGE PLAN TO WALL SECTIONS:
Where unusual grading conditions occur at the periphery of the building, they should be detailed at wall sections where they occur. These might be at basements or where the site berms up against the exterior wall.

96. GRAD'G. & DRAIN./ELEVATIONS
A. Finished grades
_____
_____
_____
_____
_____

97. _____
_____
_____
_____
_____
_____

98. GRAD'G. & DRAIN./WALL SECT.
A. Show unusual grades at bldg
periphery (basement, berms,
etc.)
_____
_____

99. _____
_____
_____
_____
_____
_____

100. _____
_____
_____
_____
_____
_____

101. _____
_____
_____
_____
_____
_____

102. _____
_____
_____
_____
_____
_____
_____

103. _____
_____
_____
_____
_____
_____

104. _____
_____
_____
_____
_____
_____

105. _____
_____
_____
_____
_____
_____

106. _____
_____
_____
_____
_____
_____

107. _____
_____
_____
_____
_____
_____

109. SITE UTILITY PLAN TO LANDSCAPING PLAN:

Where special landscape lighting is required (such as ground-mounted spot-lights shining up into trees, or small lights along walks), coordinate that the lighting is located at landscape features.

110. SITE UTILITY PLAN TO IRRIGATION PLAN:

Verify that both plans show the "tee" off for the irrigation system from the water line entering the building. Sometimes this is only shown on the Plumbing Plan. In any case, it needs to be shown somewhere that the plumbing contractor will catch it.

111. SITE UTILITY PLAN TO FOUNDATION PLAN:

Where utilities require concrete mounting pads next to the building, they are often called out on the Foundation Plan. An example might be a concrete pad for an electrical service entrance cabinet on an exterior building wall.

112. SITE UTILITY PLAN TO FLOOR PLAN:

Where utility items are next to the building, they are often shown on the first floor plan, also. An example might be a ground-mounted AC condenser with its screening walls.

108. _____
_____
_____
_____
_____
_____

109. SITE UTILITY/LANDSCAPE PL
A. Landscape lighting
_____
_____
_____
_____

110. SITE UTILITY/IRRIGATION PL
A. Water tee for irrigation
_____
_____
_____
_____

111. SITE UTILITY/FOUNDATION PL
A. Utility pads at periphery of
building
_____
_____
_____

112. SITE UTILITY/FLOOR PLAN
A. Utility items at periphery of
building
_____
_____
_____

113. _____
_____
_____
_____
_____

114. _____
_____
_____
_____
_____
_____

115. _____
_____
_____
_____
_____

116. _____
_____
_____
_____
_____

117. _____
_____
_____
_____
_____

118. _____
_____
_____
_____
_____

119. _____
_____
_____
_____
_____

126. SITE UTILITY PLAN TO PLUMBING PLAN:
   The water, sewer, and gas lines should be all shown at the same locations (including building entry location) on both plans. The line sizes should be the same on both plans. If meters are at the building, both plans should show the same locations.

127. SITE UTILITY PLAN TO ELECTRICAL POWER PLAN:
   The two should match where power and telephone enter the building. If there is an electrical service entrance section at the periphery of the building, both plans should show the same location.

120. _____

127. **SITE UTILITY/ELECT. POWER**
A. Electric power supply _____

121. _____

128. _____

122. _____

129. _____

123. _____

130. _____

125. _____

131. _____

126. **SITE UTILITY/PLUMBING**
A. Water
B. Sewer
C. Gas

132. _____

12   DISCUSSIONS

133. LANDSCAPING PLAN TO IRRIGATION PLAN:
The location of plant materials shown on the Landscape Plan should be the same as the watering devices.

137. LANDSCAPE PLAN TO DECOR/FURNITURE PLAN:
If the project has interior landscaping, this needs to be incorporated in the Decor/Furniture Plan or a new special plan made.

133. LANDSCAPE/IRRIGATION
A. Landscape watered
_____
_____
_____
_____
_____

134. _____
_____
_____
_____
_____
_____

135. _____
_____
_____
_____
_____
_____

136. _____
_____
_____
_____
_____
_____

137. LANDSCAPE/DECOR-FURN.
A. Interior landscaping
_____
_____
_____
_____

138. _____
_____
_____
_____
_____
_____

139. _____
_____
_____
_____
_____
_____
_____

140. _____
_____
_____
_____
_____
_____

141. _____
_____
_____
_____
_____
_____

142. _____
_____
_____
_____
_____
_____

143. _____
_____
_____
_____
_____
_____

144. _____
_____
_____
_____
_____
_____

156. IRRIGATION PLAN TO FOUNDATION PLAN:
Where plant material is next to the building, its watering can often cause foundation settlement or heaving problems depending on the soils involved. Soils reports often caution against this. Where this occurs, be sure sprays are directed away from building, or better yet, use drip irrigation.

145. _____

146. _____

147. _____

148. _____

149. _____

150. _____

151. _____

152. _____

153. _____

154. _____

155. _____

156. **IRRIGATION/FOUNDATION**
A. Guard against overwatering next
to foundations

159. IRRIGATION PLAN TO DECOR/FURNITURE PLAN:
If the project has interior landscaping requiring water, this needs to be shown or noted.

157. _____
_____
_____
_____
_____
_____

158. _____
_____
_____
_____
_____
_____

159. **IRRIGATION/DECOR-FURN.**
A. Interior landscaping
_____
_____
_____
_____

160. _____
_____
_____
_____
_____
_____

161. _____
_____
_____
_____
_____
_____

162. _____
_____
_____
_____
_____
_____

163. _____
_____
_____
_____
_____
_____

164. _____
_____
_____
_____
_____
_____

165. _____
_____
_____
_____
_____
_____

166. _____
_____
_____
_____
_____
_____

167. _____
_____
_____
_____
_____
_____

168. _____
_____
_____
_____
_____
_____

171. IRRIGATION PLAN TO PLUMBING PLAN:
Verify matching location and size of water tee for irrigation, on both plans. The tee is usually coming off the water line, prior to entry into the building.

172. IRRIGATION TO ELECTRICAL POWER PLAN:
Verify that the Electrical Power Plan shows a power outlet for the irrigation controller system, if used. Verify its location is the same for both plans.

178. FOUNDATION PLAN TO FLOOR PLAN:
Verify that dimensions match. Verify matching locations of perimeter walls, bearing walls, and column locations. If there are slab-on-grade changes of elevations with steps, both plans should match in this regard.

179. FOUNDATION PLAN TO DEMOLITION FLOOR PLAN:
In remodel/addition projects, determine those existing footings to be removed (and those saved and tied into).

CHECKLIST 15

169. _____

170. _____

171. **IRRIGATION/PLUMBING**
A. Water tee for irrigation

172. **IRRIGATION/ELECT. POWER**
A. Verify outlet for irrigation power

173. _____

174. _____

175. _____

176. _____

177. _____

178. **FOUNDATION/FLOOR PLAN**
A. Perimeter wall
B. Bearing wall locations
C. Column locations
D. Dimensions
E. Changes of floor elevation

179. **FOUNDATION/DEMO PLAN**
A. Existing foundations to be removed or tied into and saved

180. _____

182. FOUNDATION PLAN TO FLOOR FRAMING PLAN:
The perimeter walls and any structural walls and columns should match for size and locations.

183. FOUNDATION PLAN TO ROOF FRAMING PLAN:
For one-story buildings, the perimeter walls and any structural walls and columns should match up in size and location.

186. FOUNDATION PLAN TO BUILDING SECTIONS:
Verify foundations match both plans where building section is cut.

187. FOUNDATION PLAN TO ELEVATIONS:
If footings are to be dashed in on exterior elevations, be sure these match the Foundation Plan for proper depth.

189. FOUNDATION PLAN TO WALL SECTIONS:
At sections of exterior walls (or any other wall or column shown with footings), be sure the footings cut in section, match that called for on the Foundation Plan.

191. FOUNDATION PLAN TO HVAC PLANS:
Where there are under slab ducts and floor registers, such as for expensive homes, be sure these things are coordinated on the two plans.

192. FOUNDATION PLAN TO PLUMBING PLANS:
House plans often locate plumbing fixtures on the Foundation Plan. Plans for commercial buildings locate floor drains (and floor sinks at commercial kitchens) on the Foundation Plan to show where slopes are to be put in the concrete. Below-grade basements sometimes have sump pumps in constructed pits. When any of these are shown, be sure they are coordinated between both plans for location and number.

CHECKLIST 16

181. _____

182. FOUNDATION/FLOOR FRAME
A. Perimeter wall
B. Bearing wall locations
C. Column locations

183. FOUNDATION/ROOF FRAME
A. Perimeter wall
B. Bearing wall locations
C. Column locations

184. _____

185. _____

186. FOUNDATION/BLD'G. SECT.
A. Foundation in section

187. FOUNDATION/ELEVATIONS
A. Depth of footings in relation to grades

188. _____

189. FOUNDATION/WALL SECT.
A. Footings at wall sections

190. _____

191. FOUNDATION/HVAC
A. Under & thru slab ducts

192. FOUNDATION/PLUMBING
A. Fixtures req'g thru slab waste
B. Floor drains
C. Floor sinks
D. Basement sump pumps

Cross-Check

193. FOUNDATION PLAN TO ELECTRICAL POWER PLAN:
Should first-floor interior transformers or service entrance sections require special concrete pads, these should be shown on the Foundation Plan.

195. FOUNDATION PLAN TO SPECIAL EQUIPMENT PLAN:
Sometimes, special floor-mounted equipment requires special concrete curbs or depressions. When this occurs, both plans should match for size, height (or depth), and location. Sometimes, special curb plans are provided by the special equipment consultant.

198. FLOOR PLAN TO FLOOR PLAN:
For multistory buildings be sure perimeter walls, bearing walls, columns, and floor openings and walled shafts (for stairs, elevators, etc.) all align. Also, typically plumbing walls for toilets align from floor to floor.

199. FLOOR PLAN TO DEMOLITION PLAN:
For remodel and addition projects, existing walls and other existing items are to be dealt with (remain, removed, or modified). These issues need to be addressed and coordinated.

200. FLOOR PLAN TO DECOR-FURNITURE PLAN:
Verify that wall and door locations shown on the Floor Plan provide room for furniture layout and do not interfere with any decor items.

201. FLOOR PLAN TO REFLECTED CEILING PLAN:
Wall locations should match. Ceiling transitions and exterior overhangs shown on the Reflected Ceiling Plan are often dashed on the Floor Plan.

202. FLOOR PLAN TO FLOOR FRAMING PLAN:
Items shown on the Floor Plan that are structural or require structural framing, should match on both plans. Such items are exterior wall locations, column size and locations, interior bearing wall locations, floor openings and window (and sometimes, door) width and locations (for structural headers or lintels).

203. FLOOR PLAN TO ROOF FRAMING PLAN:
As with the Floor Framing Plan, any structural item on the floor below, that effects the roof, above, needs to be coordinated. These are exterior wall locations, column size and locations, interior bearing walls, openings for roof hatch, etc.

204. FLOOR PLAN TO ROOF PLAN:
Any item that originates on the floor below, and goes up to the roof, needs to match on both plans. Exterior walls and stairs or ladders, are examples.

193. FOUNDATION/ELECT. POWER
A. Pads for elect. equipment

194.

195. FOUND./SPECIAL EQUIP.
A. Special conc. curbs or depressions for floor-mounted equipment

196.

197.

198. FLOOR PLAN/FLOOR PLAN
A. Column locations
B. Exterior wall locations
C. Floor-to-floor openings (stairs, elevators, other shafts)

199. FLOOR PLAN/DEMO PLAN
A. Walls & items to be removed or saved & tied into

200. FLOOR PLAN/DECOR PLAN
A. Wall locations

201. FLOOR PLAN/CEILING PLAN
A. Wall locations
B. Ceiling transitions dashed on Fl. Pl.
C. Outline of roof overhangs dashed

202. FLOOR PLAN/FLOOR FRAME
A. Exterior wall locations
B. Column locations
C. Interior bearing walls
D. Floor openings
E. Window locations for headers

203. FLOOR PLAN/ROOF FRAME
A. Exterior wall locations
B. Column locations
C. Interior bearing walls
D. Roof openings/ladders
E. Window locations for headers

204. FLOOR PLAN/ROOF PLAN
A. Exterior wall locations
B. Stairs or ladders to roof

Cross-Check

205. FLOOR PLAN TO SCHEDULES:

Floor Plan location items should coordinate with schedules that give detailed information. Examples are: room names and numbers on the Room Finish Schedule; door numbers and sizes on the Door Schedule; and window sizes and designations on the Window Schedule.

206. FLOOR PLAN TO BUILDING SECTIONS:

Wall locations and sizes and types, column lines, and room names should all match between the two sheets, where appropriate at the section cut.

207. FLOOR PLAN TO ELEVATIONS:

Common items such as exterior wall, window, and door location should match between the two sheets.

208. FLOOR PLAN TO INTERIOR ELEVATIONS:

The "cut" designations on the Floor Plan should coordinate with each interior elevation detail. Interior wall, door, and window locations and sizes should match. Any special items on walls should match.

209. FLOOR PLAN TO WALL SECTIONS:

The wall types and thickness should match on both plans. If wall sections are "cut" on the Floor Plan, they should coordinate with the actual wall section details. If plan details are used (horizontal details), the "cuts" should match each plan detail.

211. FLOOR PLAN TO HVAC PLANS:

Does each room have supply and return air? If not, is this intended or a mistake? Rooms for mechanical equipment and shafts for ducts should match between each sheet.

212. FLOOR PLAN TO PLUMBING PLANS:

Do the type and location of fixtures match on both plans? Often there is a discrepancy of water closet symbols between flush tank and flush valve. Are walls thick enough for pipes and vents where fixtures back up to walls? If there is a mechanical room for a hot water heater, water softeners, or pumps, do the sizes and locations match? Are cabinets for firehose and fire extinguishers accounted for? Are standpipe locations coordinated?

213. FLOOR PLAN TO ELECTRICAL POWER PLAN:

If there is an electrical and/or telephone room, be sure there is enough room for the equipment and be sure the room location and size match on the two sheets. Where electrical panels are recessed into walls, be sure the walls are thick enough, the location does not interfere with anything else, and there is room in front of the panels. If there are vertical shafts for electrical and/or telephone, they should match between the two sheets. Where special doors or grilles are motorized, be sure power is provided.

214. FLOOR PLAN TO ELECTRICAL LIGHTING PLAN:

Wall and column locations should match between the two sheets. If there are wall-mounted light switches, be sure they do not interfere with door swings.

215. FLOOR PLAN TO SPECIAL EQUIPMENT PLAN:

Wall and column locations should match between the two sheets. Be sure there is enough room for the special equipment, especially where the equipment is side by side between walls.

205. FLOOR PLAN/SCHEDULES
   A. RM # & names
   B. Door # & size
   C. Window # & size

206. FLOOR PLAN/BLD'G. SECT'S.
   A. Wall locations
   B. Column lines
   C. Room names

207. FLOOR PLAN/ELEVATIONS
   A. Exterior wall locations
   B. Exterior window locations
   C. Exterior door locations

208. FLOOR PLAN/INTERIOR ELEV'S.
   A. Correct reference on plan
   B. Wall, door, & window locations
   C. Location of special items

209. FLOOR PLAN/WALL SECT'S.
   A. Wall types

210.

211. FLOOR PLAN/HVAC PLAN
   A. Rooms for HVAC equip.
   B. Chases for HVAC ducts
   C. Does each room have supply &
      return?

212. FLOOR PLAN/PLUMB'G. PLAN
   A. Rooms for plumbing equip
      (HWH, etc.)
   B. Fixture location & type
   C. Wall thickness for plumbing
      walls
   D. Standpipes & hose cabinets

213. FLOOR PLAN/ELECT. POWER
   A. Rooms for power & tele. equip.
   B. Chases for power & tele.
   C. Elect. panels: room in front &
      wall thickness
   D. Power for motorized doors &
      grilles

214. FLOOR PLAN/ELECT. LIGHT'G
   A. Wall locations
   B. Light switches to door swings

215. FLOOR PLAN/EQUIP. PLAN
   A. Wall locations
   B. Room for equip. between walls

216.

219. DEMOLITION PLAN TO DECOR-FURNITURE PLAN:
Where remodeling is required, any existing decor or furniture need to be accounted for as to what is to be removed and what is to be kept. This type of information needs to be coordinated between the two plans.

220. DEMOLITION PLAN TO REFLECTED CEILING PLAN:
Where remodeling is required, any existing ceilings and ceiling fixtures need to be accounted for (ceiling systems and material, ceiling fixtures, etc.). This type of information needs to be coordinated between the two plans.

221. DEMOLITION PLAN TO FLOOR FRAMING PLAN:
Where remodeling/additions are required, any existing structural framing that is saved and reused, modified or tied into, or gutted needs to be documented. This type of information needs to be coordinated between the two plans.

222. DEMOLITION PLAN TO ROOF FRAMING PLAN:
Where remodeling/additions are required, any existing structural framing that is saved and reused, modified or tied into, or gutted, needs to be documented. This type of information needs to be coordinated between the two plans.

223. DEMOLITION PLAN TO ROOF PLAN:
Where remodeling/additions are required, any existing roofs (and accessories such as hatches) that are to be saved and reused, modified or tied into, or gutted needs to be documented. This type of information needs to be coordinated between the two plans.

224. DEMOLITION PLAN TO SCHEDULES:
Where remodeling/additions are required, items such as finishes, doors, and windows that are to be saved, modified, relocated, or removed, need to be accounted for and coordinated between the two plans.

225. DEMOLITION PLAN TO BUILDING SECTIONS:
Where remodeling/additions are required, the different walls, floors, and roofs that remain or modified or removed need to be accounted for and coordinated between the two plans.

226. DEMOLITION PLAN TO ELEVATIONS:
Where remodeling/additions are required, the different walls, windows, doors, floors, and roofs reflected on the elevations, that remain or are modified or removed need to be accounted for and coordinated between the two plans.

227. DEMOLITION PLAN TO INTERIOR ELEVATIONS:
Where remodeling/additions are required, the different rooms with their walls, windows, doors, shown on the interior elevations, that are to remain, be modified, or removed need to be accounted for and coordinated between the two plans.

228. DEMOLITION PLAN TO WALL SECTIONS:
Where remodeling/additions are required, the different types of walls that remain, are modified, or removed need to be accounted for and coordinated between the two plans.

CHECKLIST 19

217. _____

218. _____

219. DEMO PLAN/DECOR PLAN
A. Items to be removed
B. Items to remain
C. Items to be relocated

220. DEMO PLAN/CEILING PLAN
A. Fixtures to be removed, saved, or relocated
B. Ceiling to be removed or saved

221. DEMO PLAN/FLOOR FRAME
A. Framing to be removed or saved

222. DEMO PLAN/ROOF FRAME
A. Framing to be removed or saved

223. DEMO PLAN/ROOF PLAN
A. Roofing to be removed or saved
B. Roof openings to be removed or saved

224. DEMO PLAN/SCHEDULES
A. Finishes to be removed, saved, or relocated
B. Doors to be removed, saved, or relocated
A. Windows to be removed, saved, or relocated

225. DEMO PLAN/BLD'G. SECT'S.
A. Construction to be removed, saved, or tied into

226. DEMO PLAN/ELEVATIONS
A. Construction to be removed, saved, or tied into

227. DEMO PLAN/INTERIOR ELEV.
A. Construction to be removed, saved, or tied into

228. DEMO PLAN/WALL SECT'S.
A. Walls to be removed, saved, or tied into

229. DEMOLITION PLAN TO MECHANICAL, PLUMBING, ELECTRICAL ROOF PLAN:

Where remodeling/additions are required, any roof-mounted equipment needs to be accounted for, as to what is to be kept, modified, or removed. This type of information needs to be coordinated between the two plans.

230. DEMOLITION PLAN TO HVAC PLANS:

Where remodeling/additions are required, any HVAC equipment and ducting needs to be accounted for, as to what is to be kept, modified, or removed. This type of information needs to be coordinated between the two plans.

231. DEMOLITION PLAN TO PLUMBING PLANS:

Where remodeling/additions are required, any plumbing fixtures and lines (water, waste, and gas) need to be accounted for as to what is to be kept, modified, or removed. This type of information needs to be coordinated between the two plans.

232. DEMOLITION PLAN TO ELECTRICAL POWER PLANS:

Where remodeling/additions are required, any electrical equipment, lines, switches, and outlets needs to be accounted for as to what is to be kept, modified, or removed. This type of information needs to be coordinated between the two plans.

233. DEMOLITION PLAN TO ELECTRICAL LIGHTING PLANS:

Where remodeling/additions are required, any electrical lighting and its power lines need to be accounted for as to what is to be kept, modified, or removed. This type of information needs to be coordinated between the two plans.

234. DEMOLITION PLAN TO SPECIAL EQUIPMENT PLANS:

Where remodeling/additions are required, any special equipment needs to be accounted for as to what is to be kept, modified, or removed. This type of information needs to be coordinated between the two plans.

235. DEMOLITION PLAN TO SPECIAL EQUIPMENT SCHEDULE:

Where remodeling/additions are required, any special equipment needs to be accounted for as to what is to be kept, modified, or removed. Use the existing schedule of equipment to aid this accounting.

236. DEMOLITION PLAN TO SPECIAL EQUIPMENT ROUGH-IN PLANS:

Where remodeling/additions are required, any special equipment needs to be accounted for as to what is to be kept, modified, or removed. Sometimes the rough-ins (water, waste, power, gas) can be reused.

238. DECOR-FURNITURE PLAN TO REFLECTED CEILING PLAN:

Where special ceilings or lighting must align with seating or decor items, below, verify that the two sheets are coordinated.

239. DECOR-FURNITURE PLAN TO FLOOR FRAMING PLAN:

Where special framing is required for built-in seating or decor items, verify that the two sheets are coordinated.

229. DEMO PLAN/MPE ROOF PLAN

A. Roof-mt'd equip. to be removed or saved

_____

_____

_____

230. DEMO PLAN/HVAC PLAN

A. HVAC to be removed, saved, or tied into

_____

_____

_____

231. DEMO PLAN/PLUMBING

A. Plumbing to be removed, saved, or tied into

B. Fixtures to be removed or saved

_____

_____

232. DEMO PLAN/ELECT. POWER

A. Electrical to be removed, saved, or tied into

_____

_____

_____

233. DEMO PLAN/ELECT. LIGHT

A. Lights to be removed or saved

_____

_____

_____

234. DEMO PLAN/EQUIP. PLAN

A. Equipment to be removed or saved

_____

_____

_____

235. DEMO PLAN/EQUIP. SCHED.

A. Equipment to be removed or saved

_____

_____

_____

236. DEMO PLAN/EQUIP. ROUGH-IN

A. Equipment to be removed or saved

_____

_____

_____

237.

_____

_____

_____

_____

_____

_____

238. DECOR PLAN/CEILING PLAN

A. Lights over special items such as tables or seats

_____

_____

_____

239. DECOR/FLOOR FRAME PLAN

A. Framing for special decor items or built-in seating

_____

_____

_____

240.

_____

_____

_____

_____

_____

_____

242. DECOR-FURNITURE PLAN TO SCHEDULES:
If interiors are part of the project, the drawings may have special schedules for decor, furniture, interior landscape, etc. If this is the case, verify that the schedules and the plans match.

243. DECOR-FURNITURE PLAN TO BUILDING SECTIONS:
If interiors are part of the project, certain built-in decor or furniture may be needed to be shown on the Building Sections. If this is the case, verify that the two sheets are coordinated.

244. DECOR-FURNITURE PLAN TO ELEVATIONS:
If "interiors" are part of the project, sometimes there is exterior decor or furniture on a patio or at a entry plaza that may be needed to be shown on the Elevations. If this is the case, verify that the two sheets are coordinated.

245. DECOR-FURNITURE PLAN TO INTERIOR ELEVATIONS:
If interiors are part of the project, certain built-in decor or furniture may be needed to be shown on the Interior Elevations. If this is the case, verify that the two sheets are coordinated.

246. DECOR-FURNITURE PLAN TO WALL SECTIONS:
If interiors are part of the project, certain built-in decor or furniture may be needed to be shown on certain Wall Sections. If this is the case, verify that the two sheets are coordinated.

249. DECOR-FURNITURE PLAN TO PLUMBING PLANS:
If interiors are part of the project, certain built-in decor (such as water fountains) may be need to be plumbed with water, waste, or gas. If this is the case, verify that the two sheets are coordinated.

250. DECOR-FURNITURE PLAN TO ELECTRICAL POWER PLANS:
Verify that electrical outlets are provided that can be used for furniture light fixtures. If interiors are part of the project, verify that electrical outlets do not interfere with furniture arrangement. Certain decor items may need dedicated power. If any of this is the case, verify that the two sheets are coordinated.

251. DECOR-FURNITURE PLAN TO ELECTRICAL LIGHTING PLANS:
If interiors are part of the project, certain built-in decor or furniture may be designed for special lighting. If this is the case, verify that the two sheets are coordinated.

252. DECOR-FURNITURE PLAN TO SPECIAL EQUIPMENT PLANS:
Be sure that furniture layout does not conflict with any special equipment.

241. _____

247. _____

242. DECOR PLAN/SCHEDULES
   A. Special schedules for decor
   B. Furniture schedules
   C. Interior plant schedules

248. _____

243. DECOR PLAN/BLD'G SECTS.
   A. Special decor items shown in section

249. DECOR PLAN/PLUMB'G PLAN
   A. Special decor needing plumbing

244. DECOR PLAN/ELEVATIONS
   A. Exterior furniture or decor shown in elevation

250. DECOR PLAN/ELECT. POWER PL
   A. Outlets for furniture lighting
   B. Furniture to outlets arrangement
   C. Power for special decor

245. DECOR PLAN/INT. ELEV'S.
   A. Decor in or on interior walls

251. DECOR PLAN/ELECT. LIGHT'G PL
   A. Lights over furniture or decor
   B. Lighting for built-in furniture
   C. Decor needing special lighting

246. DECOR PLAN/WALL SECTIONS
   A. Special built in furniture or decor

252. DECOR PLAN/EQUIP. PLAN
   A. Check for conflicts between furniture and equipment locations

256. REFLECTED CEILING PLAN TO FLOOR FRAMING PLAN:
Do any ceiling fixtures, such as chandeliers, need special framing support? Do any ceiling configurations or recesses need special framing? Where floor-to-floor openings occur, such as stairways, is this reflected on the ceiling plan and are all sheets coordinated?

257. REFLECTED CEILING PLAN TO ROOF FRAMING PLAN:
Do any ceiling fixtures, such as chandeliers, need special framing support? Do any ceiling configurations or recesses need special framing? Where floor-to-roof openings occur, such as stairways or hatches, is this reflected on the ceiling plan and are all sheets coordinated?

258. REFLECTED CEILING PLAN TO ROOF PLAN:
Where ceiling to roof openings occur, such as stairways, skylights, or hatches, is this reflected on the ceiling plan and are all sheets coordinated?

259. REFLECTED CEILING PLAN TO SCHEDULES:
Do the ceiling finishes shown on the Room Finish Schedule match what is shown on the Reflected Ceiling Plan? Check for material and height, room by room.

260. REFLECTED CEILING PLAN TO BUILDING SECTIONS:
Do the ceiling heights shown on the Reflected Ceiling Plan match those shown on the Building Sections?

261. REFLECTED CEILING PLAN TO ELEVATIONS:
Be sure that soffit heights match on both sheets and be sure that exterior windows are not higher than the interior ceilings.

262. REFLECTED CEILING PLAN TO INTERIOR ELEVATIONS:
Do the ceiling heights shown on the Reflected Ceiling Plan match those shown on the Interior Elevations?

263. REFLECTED CEILING PLAN TO WALL SECTIONS:
Do the ceiling heights shown on the Reflected Ceiling Plan match those shown on the Wall Sections? Are any special ceiling-to-wall conditions, such as coved lighting, shown on both sheets?

253. _____
_____
_____
_____
_____
_____

254. _____
_____
_____
_____
_____
_____

255. _____
_____
_____
_____
_____
_____

256. REFL. CEILING/FLOOR FRAME
A. Ceiling fixtures that need
   special framing support
B. Recessed ceiling fixtures that
   need framing room
C. Coord. floor/ceiling penetrations

257. REFL. CEILING/ROOF FRAME
A. Ceiling fixtures that need
   special framing support
B. Recessed ceiling fixtures that
   need framing room
C. Coord. roof/ceiling penetrations

258. REFL. CEILING/ROOF PLAN
A. Openings that penetrate both
   ceiling and roof such as
   skylights
_____
_____

259. REFL. CEILING/SCHEDULES
A. Ceiling materials and finishes
B. Ceiling heights
_____
_____
_____

260. REFL. CEILING/BLD'G. SECT.
A. Different ceiling heights
_____
_____
_____
_____

261. REFL. CEILING/ELEVATIONS
A. Be sure windows not higher
   than cl'g
B. Soffit elevations
_____
_____

262. REFL. CEILING/INT. ELEV'S.
A. Ceiling heights
_____
_____
_____
_____

263. REFL. CEILING/WALL SECT'S.
A. Ceiling heights
B. Special ceiling to wall
   conditions
_____
_____

264. _____
_____
_____
_____
_____
_____

265. REFLECTED CEILING PLAN TO HVAC PLANS:

Location and size of ceiling air-supply diffusers and return-air grilles should match on both plans. Usually a note on the HVAC Plan should call for the Reflected Ceiling Plan to show exact locations. It is best to not show ceiling grids on the HVAC plans.

266. REFLECTED CEILING PLAN TO PLUMBING PLANS:

If sprinklers are required and shown, the head locations should match on both plans and not interfere with any other ceiling fixture.

267. REFLECTED CEILING PLAN TO ELECTRICAL POWER PLANS:

Certain ceiling-mounted items such as sound, emergency exit signs, smoke detectors requiring power should match on both plans. Usually a note on the Electrical Power Plan should call for the Reflected Ceiling Plan to show exact locations.

268. REFLECTED CEILING PLAN TO ELECTRICAL LIGHTING PLANS:

Ceiling lighting fixture types and locations should match both plans. Usually a note on the Electrical Lighting Plan should call for the Reflected Ceiling Plan to show exact locations. It is best to not show ceiling grids on the Electrical Lighting Plan.

269. REFLECTED CEILING PLAN TO SPECIAL EQUIPMENT PLANS:

Any equipment needing special lighting, sprinklers, or hoods, should reflect these accurately for size and location, coordinated between the two sheets.

272. FLOOR FRAMING PLAN TO FLOOR FRAMING PLAN:

For multistory buildings be sure perimeter walls, bearing walls, columns, and floor openings and walled shafts (for stairs, elevators, etc.) all align.

273. FLOOR FRAMING PLAN TO ROOF FRAMING PLAN:

All exterior walls, bearing walls, columns, shafts, etc., should align between the roof and the floor below.

276. FLOOR FRAMING PLAN TO BUILDING SECTIONS:

Any framing shown in section should reflect that shown on the plan.

265. REFL. CEILING/HVAC PLAN
    A. Ceiling diffuser & return-air
       locations. Usually the HVAC plan
       should defer to the ceiling plan
       for exact locations

266. REFL. CEILING/PLUMBING PLAN
    A. Sprinkler head locations

267. REFL. CLG/ELECT. POWER PLAN
    A. Special power at ceiling for
       outlets, emergency lighting, exit
       lights, smoke detectors, etc.

268. REFL. CLG/ELECT. LIGHT'G PLAN
    A. Ceiling Light locations. Usually
       the Electrical Lighting Plan
       should defer to the ceiling plan
       for exact locations.

269. REFL. CLG/EQUIP. PLAN
    A. Lighting over equipment
    B. Sprinklers over equipment
    C. Hoods over equipment

270.

271.

272. FLR. FRAME/FLR. FRAME PLAN
    A. Align columns, bearing walls,
       and floor openings

273. FLR. FRAME/ROOF FRAME PLAN
    A. Align columns, bearing walls,
       and floor openings

274.

275.

276. FLR. FRAME/BLD'G. SECT.
    A. Show framing in section

277. FLOOR FRAMING PLAN TO ELEVATIONS:

For multistory buildings, verify elevations at tops of floors shown on the Elevations. If any exposed framing is out side of the exterior wall, that shown on the Elevations should match the Floor Framing Plan.

279. FLOOR FRAMING PLAN TO WALL SECTIONS:

Where floor framing ties into walls, the Wall Section should match that shown on the Framing Plan.

281. FLOOR FRAMING PLAN TO HVAC PLANS:

Framing for mechanical equipment and framed shafts for ducts should match between each sheet. Where there is ceiling furr down to allow for ducting, verify there is enough room.

282. FLOOR FRAMING PLAN TO PLUMBING PLANS:

Framing for equipment, such as water tanks or pumps, and framed shafts for piping, such as sprinkler risers, should match for location and size between each sheet.

283. FLOOR FRAMING PLAN TO ELECTRICAL POWER PLANS:

Framing for floor-mounted electrical and/or telephone equipment and framed shafts for power and/or telephone lines should match for location and size between each sheet.

284. FLOOR FRAMING PLAN TO ELECTRICAL LIGHTING PLANS:

Do any ceiling fixtures, such as chandeliers, need special framing support? Does any ceiling configurations or recesses need special framing?

285. FLOOR FRAMING PLAN TO SPECIAL EQUIPMENT PLANS:

Framing for floor-mounted equipment and any required special platforms or depressions in the floor should match for location and size between each sheet.

277. FLR. FRAME/ELEVATIONS

A. Denote tops of floors for multi-story

B. Exterior framing

278.

279. FLR. FRAME/WALL SECT'S.

A. Floor to wall connections

280.

281. FLR. FRAME/HVAC PLAN

A. Thru floor openings for ducts

B. Framing for floor-mt'd equip.

C. Duct furr downs

282. FLR. FRAME/PLUMBING

A. Thru floor openings for plumbing

B. Framing for floor-mt'd equip.

283. FLR. FRAME/ELECT. POWER

A. Thru floor openings for electrical

B. Framing for floor-mt'd equip.

284. FLR. FRAME/ELECT. LIGHT'G

A. Ceiling fixtures that need special framing support

B. Recessed ceiling fixtures that need framing room

C. Coord. floor/ceiling penetrations

285. FLR. FRAME/EQUIP. PLAN

A. Framing for heavy equipment

B. Recesses or platforms for equipment

286.

287.

288.

Cross-Check

289. FLOOR FRAMING PLAN TO ROOF PLAN:
Verify that roof mounted equipment is framed for. Verify that any roof openings (stairways, skylights, or hatches) is framed for. Be sure both plans are coordinated for size and number.

291. ROOF FRAMING PLAN TO BUILDING SECTIONS:
Any framing shown in section should reflect that shown on the plan.

292. ROOF FRAMING PLAN TO ELEVATIONS:
If any exposed framing is outside of the exterior walls, that shown on the elevations should match that shown on the Roof Framing Plan.

294. ROOF FRAMING PLAN TO WALL SECTIONS:
Where roof framing ties into walls, the Wall Section should match that shown on the Framing Plan.

295. ROOF FRAMING PLAN TO MPE ROOF PLAN:
Verify that roof mounted equipment is framed for. Verify that any roof openings for vertical ducts are framed for.

296. ROOF FRAMING PLAN TO HVAC PLANS:
Framing for mechanical equipment and framed shafts for ducts should match between each sheet. Where there is ceiling furred down to allow for ducting, verify there is enough room.

297. FLOOR FRAMING PLAN TO PLUMBING PLAN:
Verify that roof mounted equipment (water storage, etc.) is framed for. Verify that any roof openings for vertical plumbing lines are framed for.

289. ROOF FRAME/ROOF PLAN
  A. Roof openings
  B. Framing for roof-mt'd equipment
  _____
  _____
  _____

290. _____
  _____
  _____
  _____
  _____

291. ROOF FRAME/BLD'G. SECT'S
  A. Framing in section
  _____
  _____
  _____
  _____

292. ROOF FRAME/ELEVATIONS
  A. Exterior framing
  _____
  _____
  _____

293. _____
  _____
  _____
  _____
  _____

294. ROOF FRAME/WALL SECT'S
  A. Roof to wall conditions
  _____
  _____
  _____

295. ROOF FRAME/MPE ROOF PLAN
  A. Frame for roof-mt'd equip. &
     curbs
  B. Frame for roof opn'gs
  _____
  _____

296. ROOF FRAME/HVAC PLAN
  A. Frame for HVAC roof duct
     openings
  B. Frame for HVAC roof-mt'd equip.
  C. Frame for HVAC roof-hung equip.
  D. Framing for duct furr downs

297. ROOF FRAME/PLUMB'G PLAN
  A. Frame for plumbing roof
     openings
  B. Frame for plumb'g roof-mt'd
     equip.
  C. Frame for plumb'g roof-hung
     equip.

298. _____
  _____
  _____
  _____
  _____

299. _____
  _____
  _____
  _____
  _____

300. _____
  _____
  _____
  _____
  _____

305. ROOF PLAN TO BUILDING SECTIONS:
Verify correct roof heights between the two sheets.

306. ROOF PLAN TO ELEVATIONS:
Elevations typically have the profile of the roof dashed if the exterior wall has a parapet; otherwise the edge of roof will be shown. Verify correct roof heights between the two sheets. Where there are roof scuppers or down spouts, be sure these are coordinated between the two sheets.

308. ROOF PLAN TO WALL SECTIONS:
Where roof attaches to or overhangs wall, verify correct roof connections and heights between the two sheets.

309. ROOF PLAN TO MPE ROOF PLAN:
Verify that roof-mounted equipment is shown at the same size and location between the two sheets. Technically, the MPE Roof Plan should be looking down on the top of the equipment, while the Roof Plan should show the equipment curbs or platforms (with the outline of the above equipment dashed). Drainage around the platforms or curbs should be allowed for by "crickets," etc., shown on the Roof Plan. If there is roof lighting, verify that it is powered on the MPE Roof Plan and both plans are coordinated for the number and location of lights. If there is no MPE Roof Plan, look for the equivalent information on HVAC, plumbing, and electrical plans.

CHECKLIST 26

301. _____

302. _____

303. _____

304. _____

305. **ROOF PL./BUILD'G. SECT'S.**
A. Roof in section at right heights

306. **ROOF PLAN/ELEVATIONS**
A. Dash roof outline on elevations
B. Be sure scuppers & D.S. align

307. _____

308. **ROOF PLAN/WALL SECT'S.**
A. Roof to parapet or facia conditions

309. **ROOF PLAN/MPE ROOF PL.**
A. Align and account for all roof-mt'd equip. on both plans
B. On roof plan allow for drainage around roof-mt'd equip.
C. Roof lights

310. _____

311. _____

312. _____

319. SCHEDULES TO ELEVATIONS:
Verify that door and window designations and sizes, called for on the Door Schedule and Window Schedule, match that shown on the Elevations.

320. SCHEDULES TO INTERIOR ELEVATIONS:
Verify that door and window designations and sizes, called for on the Door Schedule and Window Schedule, match that shown on the Interior Elevations.

323. SCHEDULES TO HVAC PLANS:
Use Room Finish Schedule as an organized list of the rooms to check against the HVAC Plans to be sure each room has supply and return air. If not, often the HVAC Plans call for its door to be "undercut." This notation should be on the Door Schedule.

313. _____
_____
_____
_____
_____
_____
_____

319. SCHEDULES/ELEVATIONS
A. Door # and sizes
B. Window # and sizes
_____
_____
_____

314. _____
_____
_____
_____
_____
_____

320. SCHEDULES/INTER. ELEV'S
A. Door # and sizes
B. Window # and sizes
_____
_____
_____

315. _____
_____
_____
_____
_____
_____

321. _____
_____
_____
_____
_____
_____
_____

316. _____
_____
_____
_____
_____
_____

322. _____
_____
_____
_____
_____
_____

317. _____
_____
_____
_____
_____
_____
_____

323. SCHEDULES/HVAC PLAN
A. Use Rm. Fin. Sch. to check all
rooms for supply and return air
B. Dr. Sch. to HVAC for undercuts
req'd
_____

318. _____
_____
_____
_____
_____

324. _____
_____
_____
_____
_____
_____

331. BUILDING SECTIONS TO ELEVATIONS:

Verify that exterior walls align and roof and parapet heights are correct so that the two sheets are coordinated. Verify building section cuts are correct on Elevations.

332. BUILDING SECTIONS TO INTERIOR ELEVATIONS:

Verify that the two sheets match as to room widths and heights where the section is "cut." Sometimes, it is best to simply show the Interior Elevations in the Building Section as a combination.

333. BUILDING SECTIONS TO WALL SECTIONS:

Verify that the two sheets match, where Wall Sections are a "blow-up" of walls shown on the Building Section. Verify that the "cut" designations or "flags" match.

334. BUILDING SECTIONS TO MPE ROOF PLAN:

Where required, verify tops of equipment are not higher than parapets. City zoning ordinances often require that roof-mounted equipment be "screened."

325. _____

326. _____

327. _____

328. _____

329. _____

330. _____

331. BLD'G. SECT'S./ELEVATIONS
A. Align walls
B. Align heights
C. Section cuts

332. BLD'G. SECT'S./INTER. ELEV'S.
A. Use Building Sections as part of the Interior Elevations
B. Align heights

333. BLD'G. SECT'S./WALL SECT'S.
A. "Flag" and blow up

334. BLD'G. SECT'S./MPE ROOF PL.
A. Plot equip heights if parapets or screens are required to block view of equipment

335. _____

336. _____

343. ELEVATIONS TO INTERIOR ELEVATIONS:
Exterior doors and windows should match for size and location where Interior Elevations are the inside face of exterior walls.

344. ELEVATIONS TO WALL SECTIONS:
Check to be sure that exterior Wall Sections are "cut" or "flagged" properly on the Elevations.

345. ELEVATIONS TO MPE ROOF PLAN:
Where required, verify tops of equipment are not higher than parapets. City zoning ordinances often require that roof-mounted equipment be "screened."

346. ELEVATIONS TO HVAC PLANS:
Verify the location of any exterior vents or grilles on the Elevations, called for by the HVAC Plans.

347. ELEVATIONS TO PLUMBING PLANS:
Verify the location of any exterior hose bibs, meters, exposed pipes on the Elevations, called for by the Plumbing Plans.

348. ELEVATIONS TO ELECTRICAL POWER PLANS:
Verify the location of any exterior panels or cabinets on the Elevations, called for by the Electrical Power Plans.

337. _____
_____
_____
_____
_____
_____

338. _____
_____
_____
_____
_____
_____

339. _____
_____
_____
_____
_____
_____

340. _____
_____
_____
_____
_____
_____

341. _____
_____
_____
_____
_____
_____

342. _____
_____
_____
_____
_____
_____

343. ELEVATIONS/INTER. ELEV'S.
A. Align exterior doors
B. Align exterior windows
_____
_____
_____

344. ELEVATIONS/WALL SECT'S.
A. "Flag" all "cuts" as required
_____
_____
_____
_____

345. ELEVATIONS/MPE ROOF PLAN
A. Be sure all roof-mt'd equip. is
   screened, if required
_____
_____
_____

346. ELEVATIONS/HVAC PLAN
A. Wall grilles or louvers
_____
_____
_____
_____

347. ELEVATIONS/PLUMB'G. PLAN
A. Exterior plumbing items such as
   hose bibbs, meters, exposed
   lines
_____
_____

348. ELEVATIONS/ELECT. POWER
A. Exterior electrical, such as panels
_____
_____
_____
_____

349. ELEVATIONS TO ELECTRICAL LIGHTING PLANS:
Verify the location of any exterior wall lights on the Elevations called for by the Electrical Lighting Plans. Sometimes the Electrical Lighting Plans defer to the Elevations for exact locations and heights.

354. INTERIOR ELEVATIONS TO WALL SECTIONS:
Check to be sure that interior Wall Sections are "cut" or "flagged" properly on the Interior Elevations.

356. INTERIOR ELEVATIONS TO HVAC PLANS:
Verify that wall grilles are properly shown on the Interior Elevations where called for on the HVAC Plans.

357. INTERIOR ELEVATIONS TO PLUMBING PLANS:
Verify that plumbing fixtures (lavs, sinks, urinals, water closets) are properly shown on the Interior Elevations where called for on the Plumbing Plans.

358. INTERIOR ELEVATIONS TO ELECTRICAL PLANS:
Verify that wall electrical panels are properly shown on the Interior Elevations where called for on the Electrical Plans.

359. INTERIOR ELEVATIONS TO ELECTRICAL LIGHTING PLANS:
Verify that wall lighting fixtures are properly shown on the Interior Elevations where called for on the Electrical Lighting Plans. Sometimes the Electrical Lighting Plans defer to the Interior Elevations for exact locations and heights.

360. INTERIOR ELEVATIONS TO SPECIAL EQUIPMENT PLANS:
Sometimes the special equipment is shown in elevation on the Interior Elevations. If this is done, be sure that shown on the Interior Elevations, matches that shown on the Special Equipment Plans. Sometimes the special equipment is shown in elevation on the Special Equipment drawings.

349. ELEVATIONS/ELECT. LIGHT'G.
A. Exterior wall lights
_____
_____
_____
_____
_____

350. _____
_____
_____
_____
_____
_____

351. _____
_____
_____
_____
_____
_____

352. _____
_____
_____
_____
_____
_____

353. _____
_____
_____
_____
_____
_____

354. INTER. ELEV'S./WALL SECT'S.
A. "Flag" special "cut" as required
_____
_____
_____
_____

355. _____
_____
_____
_____
_____
_____
_____

356. INTER. ELEV'S./HVAC PLAN
A. Wall air supply grilles
_____
_____
_____
_____

357. INTER. ELEV'S./PLUMB'G. PLAN
A. Plumbing fixtures in elevation
_____
_____
_____
_____

358. INTER. ELEV'S./ELECT. POWER
A. Electrical panels in elevation
_____
_____
_____
_____

359. INTER. ELEV'S/ELECT. LGT'G.
A. Wall lights
_____
_____
_____
_____

360. INTER. ELEV'S./EQUIP. PLAN
A. Equip. in elevation (often
   shown on special equip.
   drawings)
_____
_____

Cross-Check

361.

362.

363.

364.

365.

366.

367.

368.

369.

370.

371.

372.

Cross-Check

373. MPE ROOF PLAN TO HVAC PLANS:
Verify that both plans align for roof-mounted equipment locations and through-the-roof openings for ducts.

374. MPE ROOF PLAN TO PLUMBING PLANS:
Verify that both plans align for any roof-mounted equipment locations and through-the-roof openings for pipes. Verify roof-mounted equipment is plumbed, if required.

375. MPE ROOF PLAN TO ELECTRICAL POWER PLANS:
Verify that roof-mounted equipment and any parapet signage have power.

376. MPE ROOF PLAN TO ELECTRICAL LIGHTING PLANS:
Verify that any roof-mounted lights have power.

377. MPE ROOF PLAN TO SPECIAL EQUIPMENT PLAN:
Verify that any roof-mounted equipment (such as exhaust fans) that serves special equipment below, align.

380. HVAC PLAN TO HVAC PLAN:
If the project is a multistoried building, with vertical ducts, from floor to floor, verify they align.

381. HVAC PLANS TO PLUMBING PLANS:
Verify that HVAC equipment is plumbed (water supply, etc.) as required. Verify that plumbing fixtures (such as hot water heater) are vented, if required.

382. HVAC PLANS TO ELECTRICAL POWER PLANS:
Verify that HVAC equipment is powered as required. Verify that electrical equipment (such as transformers) is vented or ventilated, if required.

383. HVAC PLANS TO ELECTRICAL LIGHTING PLANS:
Verify that the HVAC diffusers and return air grilles in the ceiling do not interfere with the ceiling-mounted lights.

384. HVAC PLANS TO SPECIAL EQUIPMENT PLANS:
Verify that special equipment is vented or ventilated, if required.

373. MPE ROOF PL/HVAC PLAN
A. Roof-mt'd. equip. & openings align

374. MPE ROOF PL/PLUMB'G.
A. Plumb roof-mounted equip. as req'd.

375. MPE ROOF PL/ELECT. POWER
A. Power roof-mounted equip. as req'd.
B. Power for parapet signs

376. MPE ROOF PL/ELECT. LIT'G.
A. Roof lighting

377. MPE ROOF PL/EQUIP. PL
A. HVAC equip. for equip. below such as exhaust fans

378.

379.

380. HVAC PLAN/HVAC PLAN
A. Vertical ducts

381. HVAC PL/PLUMB'G PL
A. Plumb HVAC equip. as req'd.
B. Ventilation of plumbing equip. as req'd., such as gas HWH

382. HVAC PL/ELECT. POWER
A. Power to HVAC equip.
B. Vent electrical equip.

383. HVAC PL/ELECT. LIGHTING
A. HVAC ceiling diffusers & RAGs do not interfere w/elect. ceiling lights

384. HVAC PL/EQUIP. PLAN
A. Ventilation to special equip. as req'd.

387. PLUMBING PLAN TO PLUMBING PLAN:
Where the project is multistoried, verify that vertical supply and waste lines align between floors.

388. PLUMBING PLANS TO ELECTRICAL POWER PLANS:
Verify that power is to plumbing equipment such as pumps and water heaters, etc.

391. PLUMBING PLANS TO SPECIAL EQUIPMENT SCHEDULE:
Verify that plumbing (water, waste, gas) is to special equipment, as required.

392. PLUMBING PLANS TO SPECIAL EQUIPMENT ROUGH-IN PLAN:
Verify that plumbing (water, waste, gas) is to special equipment, as required, where plumbing rough-in plan shows.

393. ELECTRICAL POWER PLAN TO ELECTRICAL POWER PLAN:
Where the project is multistory, verify the vertical shafts for power supply (and telephone) between floors, align.

394. ELECTRICAL POWER PLANS TO ELECTRICAL LIGHTING PLANS:
Verify that light fixtures are powered.

396. ELECTRICAL POWER PLANS TO SPECIAL EQUIPMENT SCHEDULE:
Verify that power is to special equipment, as required.

385. _____
_____
_____
_____
_____
_____

386. _____
_____
_____
_____
_____
_____

387. PLUMB'G PL/PLUMB'G PL
A. Vertical supply & waste lines,
align
_____
_____
_____
_____

388. PLUMB'G/ELECT. POWER
A. Power to plumbing equip. as
req'd (such as pumps, HWHs,
etc.)
_____
_____

389. _____
_____
_____
_____
_____
_____

390. _____
_____
_____
_____
_____
_____

391. PLUMB'G/EQUIP. SCHEDULE
A. Plumbing requirements for special equip. (CW, HW, waste, gas)
_____
_____
_____

392. PLUMB'G/EQUIP. ROUGH-IN
A. Plumbing requirements for special equip. (CW, HW, waste, gas)
_____
_____
_____

393. ELECT. POWER/ELECT. POWER
A. Vertical shafts for power
_____
_____
_____
_____
_____

394. ELECT. POWER/ELECT. LT'G.
A. Power to lights
_____
_____
_____
_____
_____

395. _____
_____
_____
_____
_____
_____

396. ELECT. POWER/EQUIP. SCHED.
A. Power to special equipment
_____
_____
_____
_____

397. ELECTRICAL POWER PLANS TO SPECIAL EQUIPMENT ROUGH-IN PLAN:
Verify that power is to special equipment, as required, where electrical rough-in plan shows.

399. ELECTRICAL LIGHTING PLANS TO SPECIAL EQUIPMENT PLANS:
Where special equipment has specific lighting, verify the two plans are coordinated.

404. SPECIAL EQUIPMENT PLAN TO SPECIAL EQUIPMENT SCHEDULE:
Special equipment items on the plan should match the schedule.

405. SPECIAL EQUIPMENT PLAN TO SPECIAL EQUIPMENT ROUGH-IN PLAN:
Special equipment items should align on both plans.

407. SPECIAL EQUIPMENT SCHEDULE TO SPECIAL EQUIPMENT ROUGH-IN PLAN:
Special equipment utilities (water, waste, power, and gas) should match on both plans.

397. ELECT. POWER/EQ. ROUGH-IN

A. Power to special equipment

398.

399. ELECT. LIGHT'G./EQ. PLAN

A. Lighting required for special equip.

400.

401.

402.

403.

404. EQUIP. PL/EQUIP. SCHED.

A. Items on plan should match schedule

405. EQ. PLAN/EQ. ROUGH-IN

A. Items on plan should match rough-in

406.

407. EQ. SCHED/EQ. ROUGH-IN

A. Items on schedule should match rough-in

408.

Chapter 4

Common Errors

The past chapter listed a lot of potential coordination conflicts, some minor and some major. This chapter will discuss a few major and common errors.

A major coordination error is a problem that can cause major redesign in the CD phase or major demolition and reconstruction during construction, depending on when the error comes to light. These types of coordination errors are best resolved during the DD phase. Past that, they become major problems.

Common errors may not be major but need special care because they can occur frequently on every project.

1. IS THERE ENOUGH ROOM BETWEEN THE ROOF OR FLOOR AND THE CEILING, BELOW?

Past the DD phase, this can be a major disaster. So, this is best planned for in that phase and then back checked in the CD phase. For many building types the roof or floor to ceiling (below) "sandwich" is packed with all kinds of "goodies." So, the sandwich needs to be thick enough for everything to fit. But at the same time, the higher a building is, the more expensive it becomes. This is exponential for multi-story buildings. Besides cost, there may be other reasons for keeping the building as low as possible, such as legal requirements. So this is a problem that requires careful consideration. The "goodies" in the "sandwich," going from top to bottom, include the structural deck and then the structural members below. Below this are the HVAC ducts and plumbing lines (water, waste, gas, and sprinklers). The waste lines are sloped (about 1%), which over a long distance will have an effect on height. After these come recessed light fixtures, typically 6- to 8-in above the bottom of the ceiling. Finally, there is the ceiling material. Usually an acoustical tile ceiling grid system is about an inch thick. A typical floor (or roof) to ceiling space with typical dimensions is shown below. Use this as a starter, but check the dimensions for each project, as they can vary.

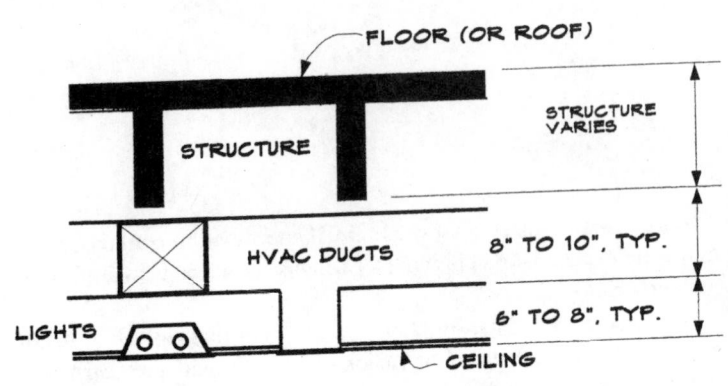

FLOOR TO CEILING SPACE

Usually the critical (variable) elements are the structural system and the ducts. The structural system will have a large effect on the total depth. Structural systems with the least depth would be a plywood deck with joists of short span for wood-frame buildings or a system of concrete-filled metal deck with wide-flange steel beams (if fireproofing is needed, add for this, typically 1 in for spray on) will require the least depth. Often deeper structural systems (such as trusses or open web joists) are less costly. Sometimes duct work can be run along the line of the structure (between the structural members). If the system is an open truss or joist, the ducts can often be run through them. If the structural system is for a roof, it might be sloped (usually at least 2% for a "flat" roof), which is another consideration.

This can become very messy and confusing. The best approach is to check a few critical points and very likely the rest is OK. Check where the deepest duct crosses the deepest girder. In the case of a sloped roof deck, this is often at the high point. If so, then check a low point of the roof even though the ducts may not be so deep.

A careful design of—and then back check for—this problem must be done, even though it becomes complicated and may not be enjoyable.

2. DO DIMENSIONS FROM ONE PLAN TO ANOTHER MATCH?

The best thing to do is to not duplicate dimensions, but sometimes this cannot be avoided, as in the floor plan and the foundation plan. A careful planning of the dimensions in the beginning and back checks will solve a lot of potential problems.

3. ARE BACKGROUNDS THE SAME THROUGHOUT THE PLANS?

It goes without saying that all horizontal plans must show the same walls (exterior and interior), the same column (and grid) locations, the same door locations and swings, the same window locations and sizes, and finally, the same building orientation. But it does need to be said, because often the backgrounds are in conflict, for a variety of reasons. The most common reason is usually due to a change of design affecting the basic plan. It is best to avoid these type of changes in the CD phase, but when they must be made, carry them out completely. A typical scenario is that for whatever reason, the architect must make some kind of background change. This is sent to the consulting engineer. But, because the engineer is so involved in designing his or her part of the building, the change is buried with other paper and the engineer forgets to give it to the drafter. The result is a light switch behind a door or a ceiling diffuser where a light is. This is why it is so important for the architect to back check. Development of the drawings and ease of back checking is always easier if the plans are all of the same scale and orientation.

4. IS ROOF-MOUNTED EQUIPMENT COORDINATED?

Most small and medium-size buildings have roof-mounted HVAC equipment. The mechanical engineer (and sometimes the specialty equipment designer) locates roof-mounted equipment at the location best suited for him or her, not taking into consideration framing support and roof drainage around the equipment. The mechanical engineer needs to supply information, such as the equipment size, location, weight, and required opening size. The architect needs to consult with the structural engineer concerning proper support and framing for any required openings. After further study, the equipment might have to be moved to a better location. In the end, the HVAC Plan must align with the MPE Roof Plan (if there is one), with the Roof Plan (showing the curbs and drainage pattern), and with the structural Roof Framing Plan for support and framing of openings. If ducts go directly to the ceiling for some reason, then the Reflected Ceiling Plan is involved. Often the mechanical and structural plans are not coordinated, which must be resolved by someone in the field.

5. HAS THE ARCHITECT BACK CHECKED THE CONSULTANTS?

The architect, no matter how extensively trained, will not know the specialized engineering design of his or her consultants (although the architect often gains a feel for proper sizes, over time). Still, he or she is the one in charge of the allocation of physical space. A 30″ duct cannot go through joists at 2′ on center and a light cannot be where a diffuser is. The architect cannot just do the "A" sheets and let the consultants do theirs. He or she has to do the drawings and coordinate what the consultants do. The architect need not back check their designs, except to the extent that they do not physically interfere with one another. Not doing this probably leads to the most problems with a set of plans.

Chapter 5

Exercise

This chapter deals with one hypothetical small building design project that has coordination errors in the drawings. Perhaps you are the principal of a small firm and at the beginning of the CD phase. You turned the project over to your drafter and now are checking the work. Or, perhaps you are a project architect that has just taken over the project or have been asked to do an independent check.

In any case, the working drawings are pretty evenly developed at about 50%. The specifications are not yet started but a Table of Contents has been made listing the sections intended to be used.

The project is a small existing church with an existing sanctuary and a small existing classroom building. The project is to add a new multipurpose room building. The classroom building will be remodeled by redoing the minister's office and making one of the classrooms into a new kitchen.

The list of the working drawings to date, and the corresponding Cross-Check generic drawings that might apply in a coordination check, are listed below:

Working Drawings	*Cross-check*
EC-1 thru EC-9	Survey
(Existing Conditions)	

Working Drawings	Cross-check
A-1 (Site Plan)	Site Plan, Demo Site Plan, Site Utility Plan, Landscape Plan, Irrigation Plan
A-2 (Foundation Plan)	Foundation Plan
A-3 (Floor Plan)	Floor Plan, Demo Plan
A-4 (Decor/Furniture Plan)	Decor/Furniture Plan
A-5 (Reflected Ceiling Plan)	Reflected Ceiling Plan
A-6 (Roof Framing Plan)	Roof Framing Plan
A-7 (Roof Plan)	Roof Plan
A-8 (Schedules)	Schedules
A-9 (Building Section)	Building Sections
A-10 (Elevations)	Elevations
A-11 (Interior Elevations)	Interior Elevations
A-12 (Wall Sections)	Wall Sections
M-1 (HVAC Plan)	MPE Roof Plan, HVAC Plans
P-1 (Plumbing Plan)	MPE Roof Plan, Plumbing Plans
E-1 (Electrical Power Plan)	Electrical Power Plans
E-2 (Electrical Lighting Plan)	Electrical Lighting Plan
K-1 (Kitchen plan)	Special Equipment Plan, Schedules and Rough-in's

The "Existing Conditions" drawings are a compilation of drawings from the original plans of the building. The list of anticipated specifications sections are on pages 102 through 110.

Using the Cross-Check system in Chapter 3, check for the coordination of the drawings and specifications only. Other checks for completeness, code, etc., have been or will be done, but are not to be done now, and are not part of this exercise.

Use the Cross-Check system anyway you feel convenient to find coordination errors in the drawings. Use the CSI Format in Appendix A on page 153 as you go through the drawings to see what things are, or are not in this project, to redline the Table of Contents.

Chapter Five

In the case of the project architect scenario, your boss has promised you lunch if you find 10 errors and dinner if you find 20 errors!

As you proceed, take note of the different type of errors. All errors are not good, but some are much worse than others. Some are like "typos," but others are poor planning from the beginning.

The "answers" are on pages 131 through 151. Don't peek!

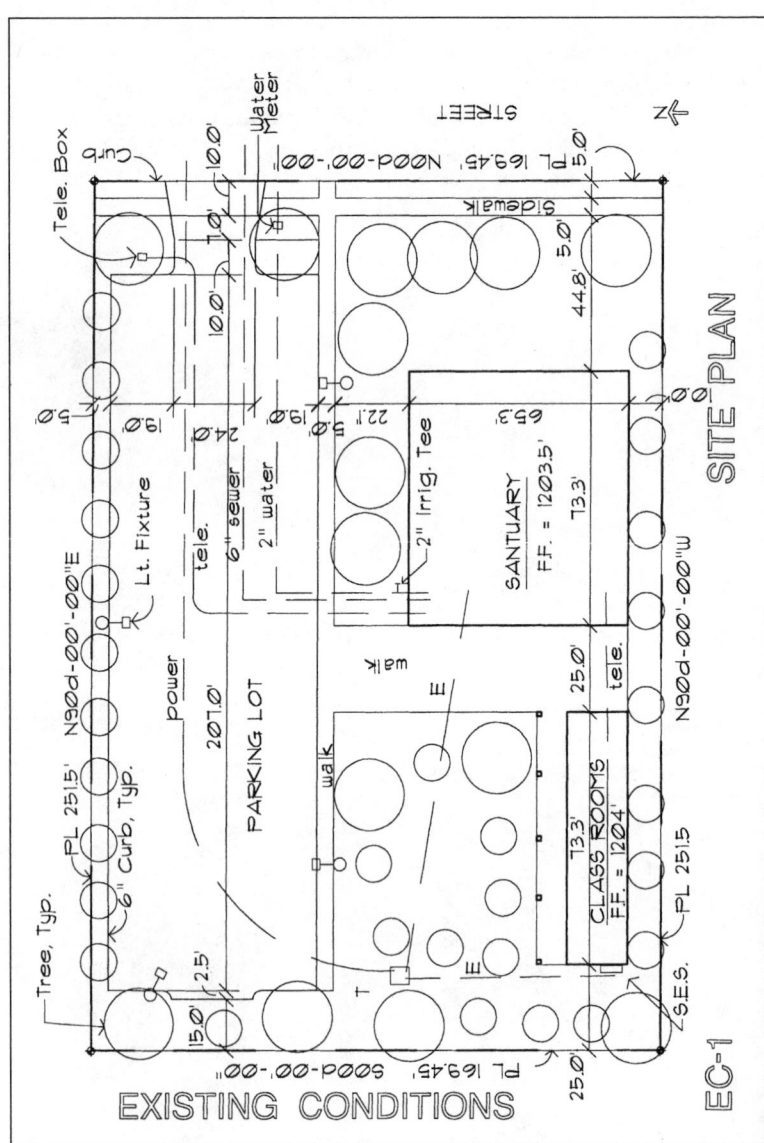

SITE PLAN

EXISTING CONDITIONS

EC-1

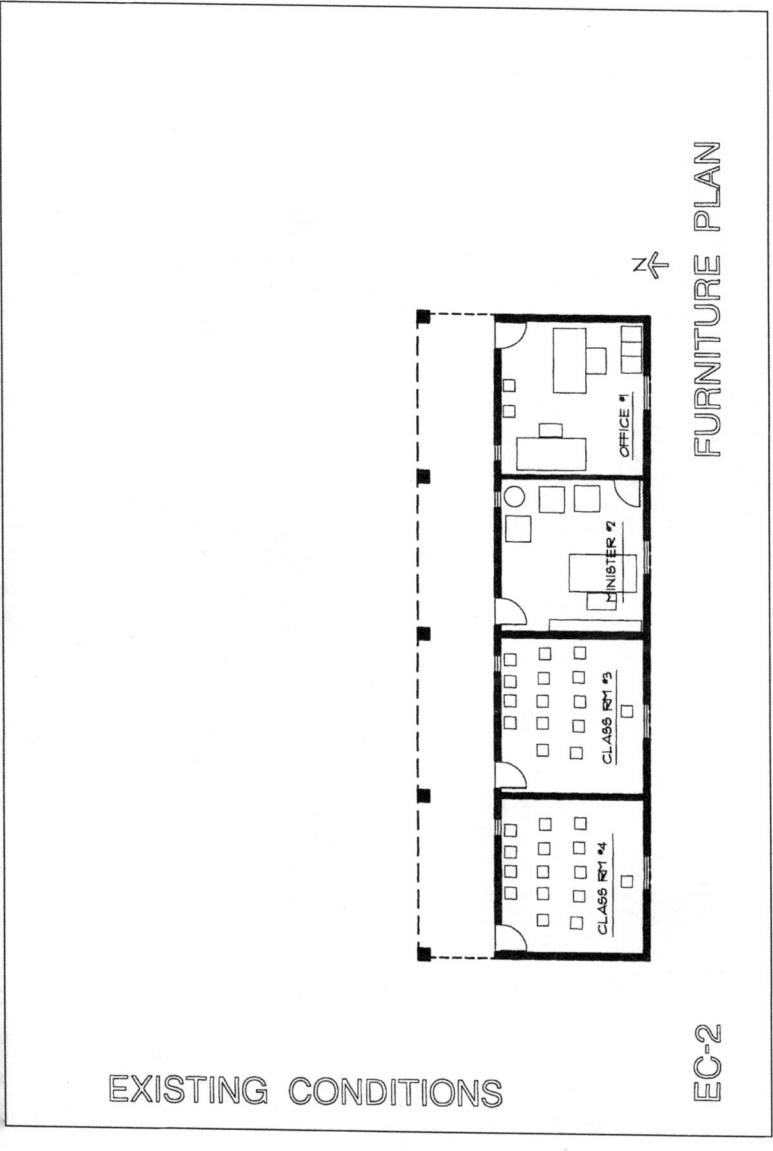

FURNITURE PLAN

N

OFFICE #1

MINISTER #2

CLASS RM #3

CLASS RM #4

EXISTING CONDITIONS

EC-2

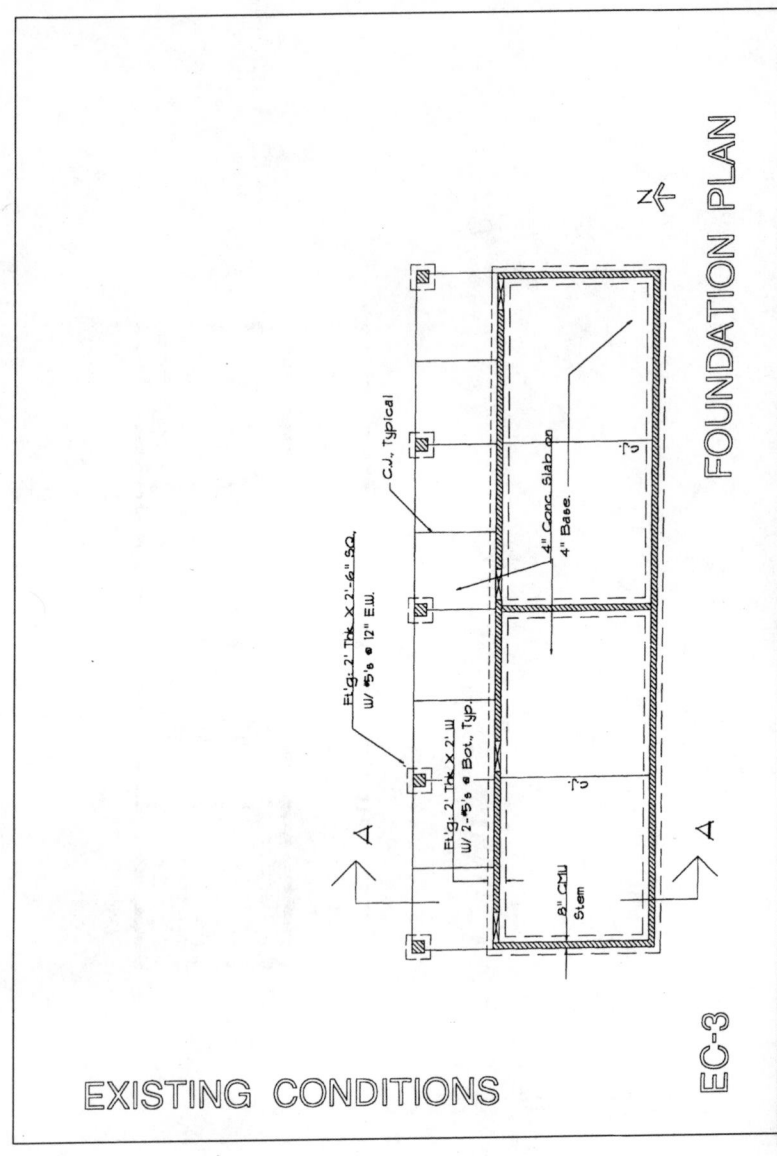

Ftg.-2' Thk × 2'-6" SQ.
w/ #5's @ 12" E.W.

C.J. Typical

Ftg.-2' Thk × 2' W.
w/ 2-#5's @ Bot., Typ.

4" Conc. Slab on
4" Base.

8" CMU
Stem

A

A

FOUNDATION PLAN

EXISTING CONDITIONS

EC-3

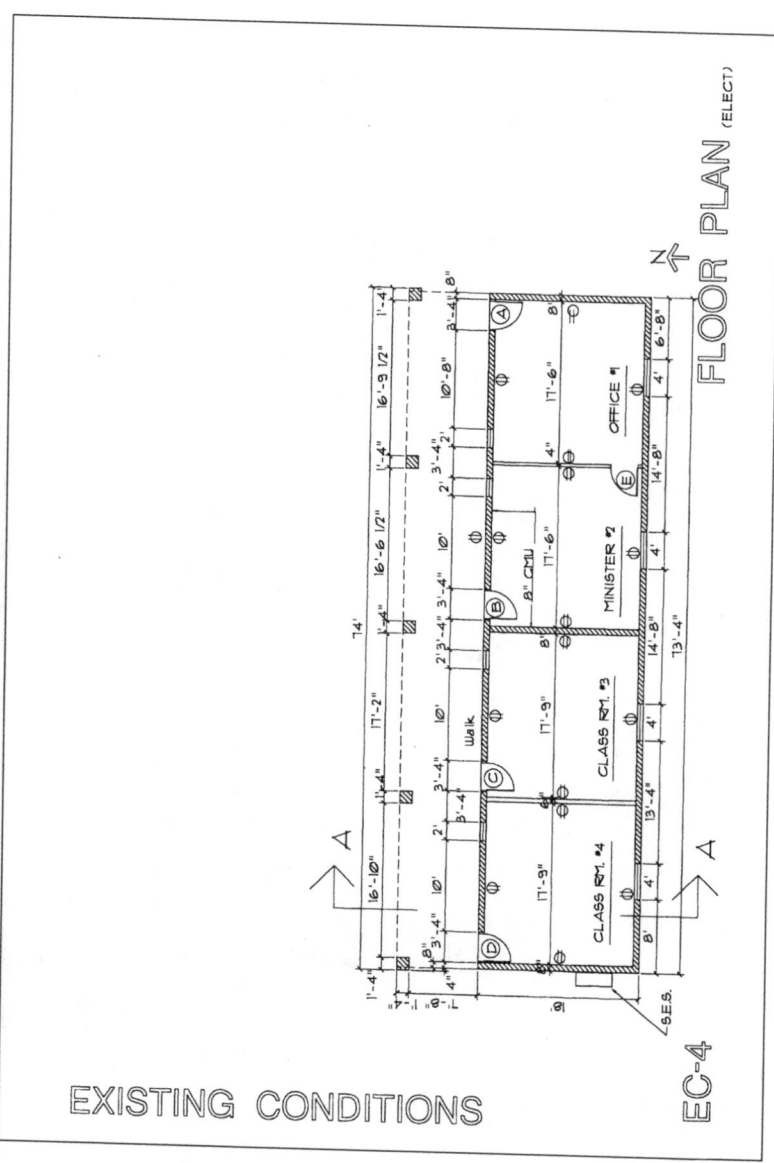

EXISTING CONDITIONS

FLOOR PLAN (ELECT)

EC-4

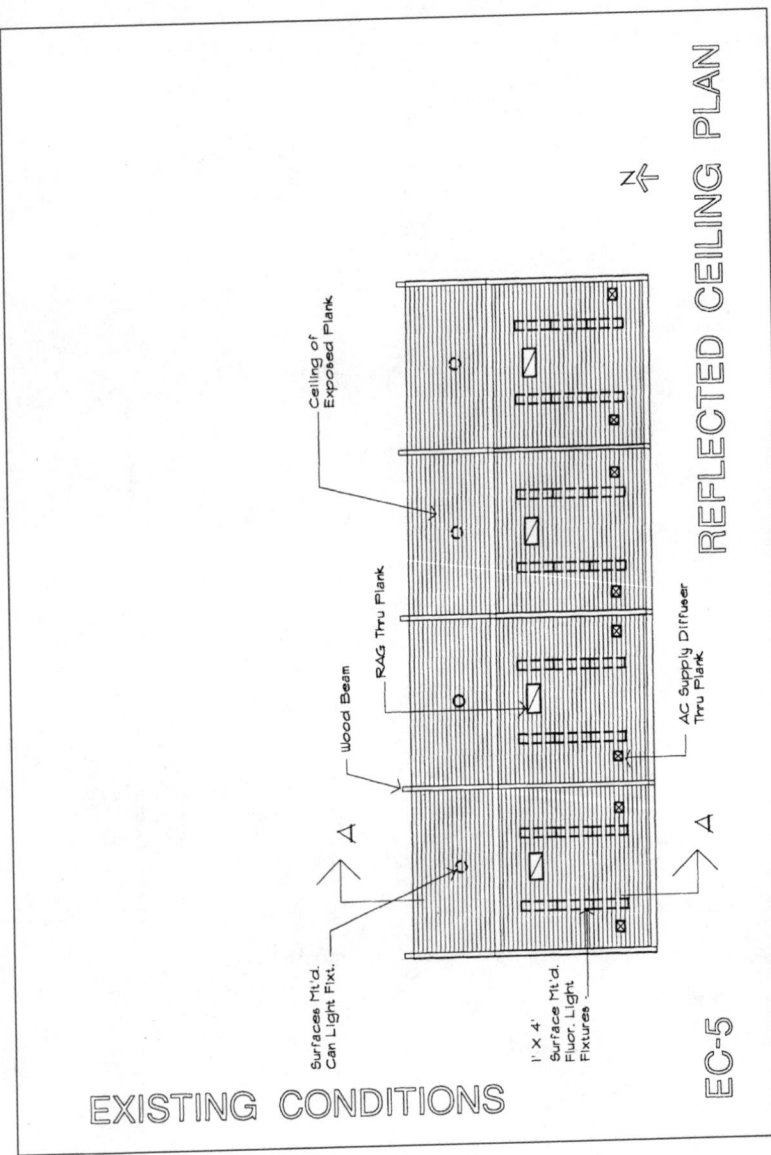

EXISTING CONDITIONS

Ceiling of Exposed Plank

RAG Thru Plank

Wood Beam

AC Supply Diffuser Thru Plank

Surfaces Mt'd. Can Light Fixt.

1' X 4' Surface Mt'd. Fluor. Light Fixtures

EC-5

N

REFLECTED CEILING PLAN

EXISTING CONDITIONS

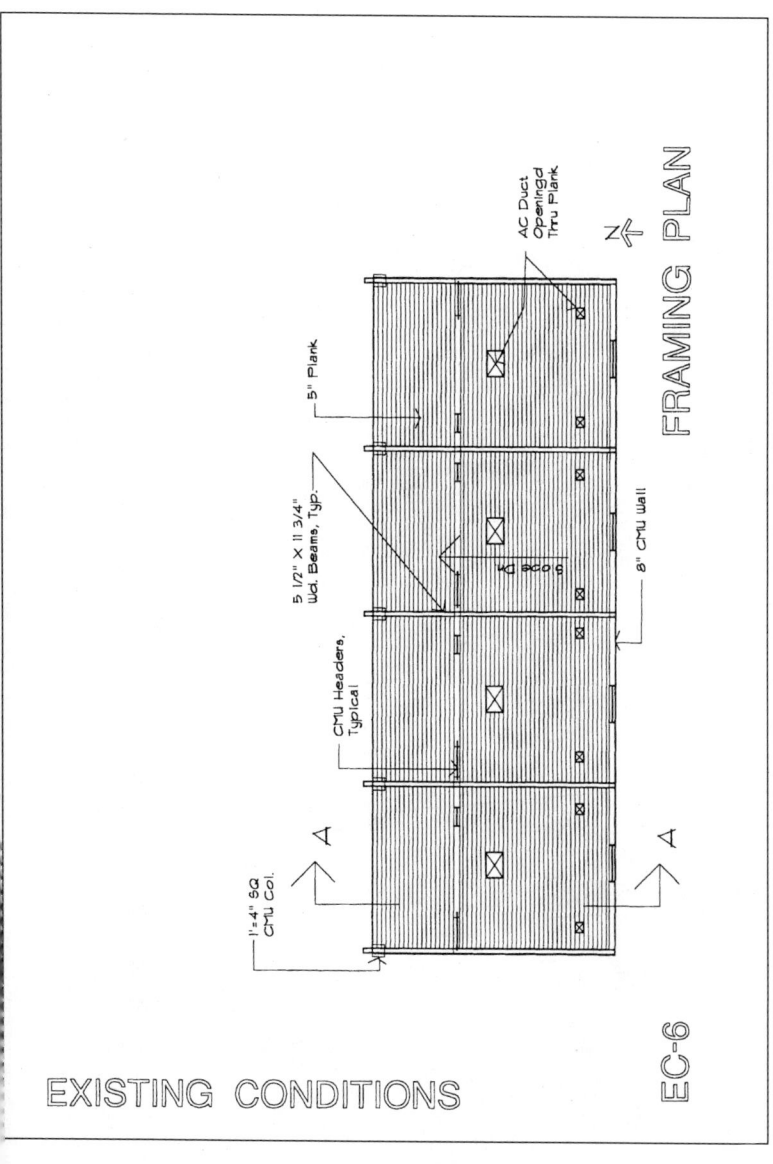

1'-4" SQ CMU Col.

CMU Headers, Typical

5 1/2" X 11 3/4" Wd. Beams, Typ.

5" Plank

AC Duct Openings Thru Plank

8" CMU Wall

A

A

N

FRAMING PLAN

EC-6

Exercise

107

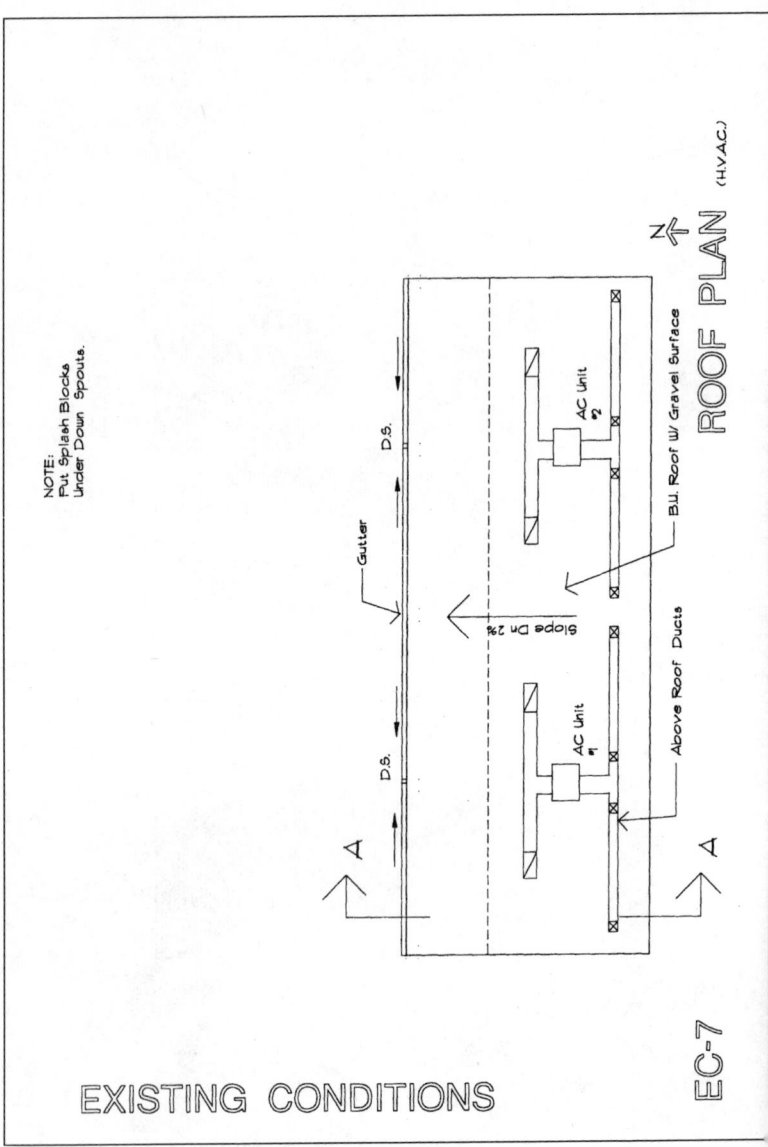

NOTE:
Put Splash Blocks
Under Down Spouts.

D.S.

Gutter

D.S.

Slope Dn 2%

AC Unit #2

AC Unit #1

B.U. Roof W/ Gravel Surface

Above Roof Ducts

A

A

N

ROOF PLAN (H.V.A.C.)

EC-7

EXISTING CONDITIONS

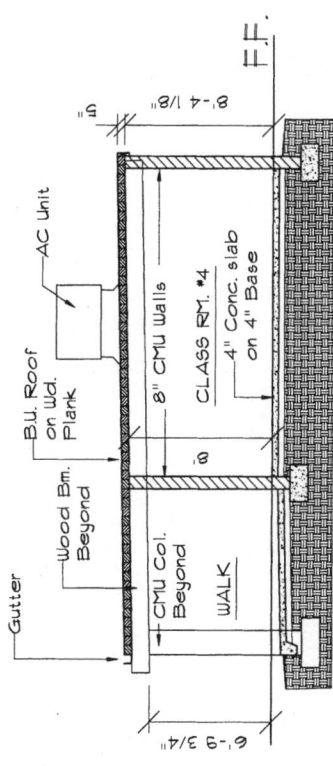

BUILDING SECTION

Gutter

Wood Bm. Beyond

B.U. Roof on Wd. Plank

AC Unit

CMU Col. Beyond

8" CMU Walls

CLASS RM. #4

8'

WALK

4" Conc. slab on 4" Base

F.F.

5"

8'-4 1/8"

6'-9 3/4"

EXISTING CONDITIONS

EC-8

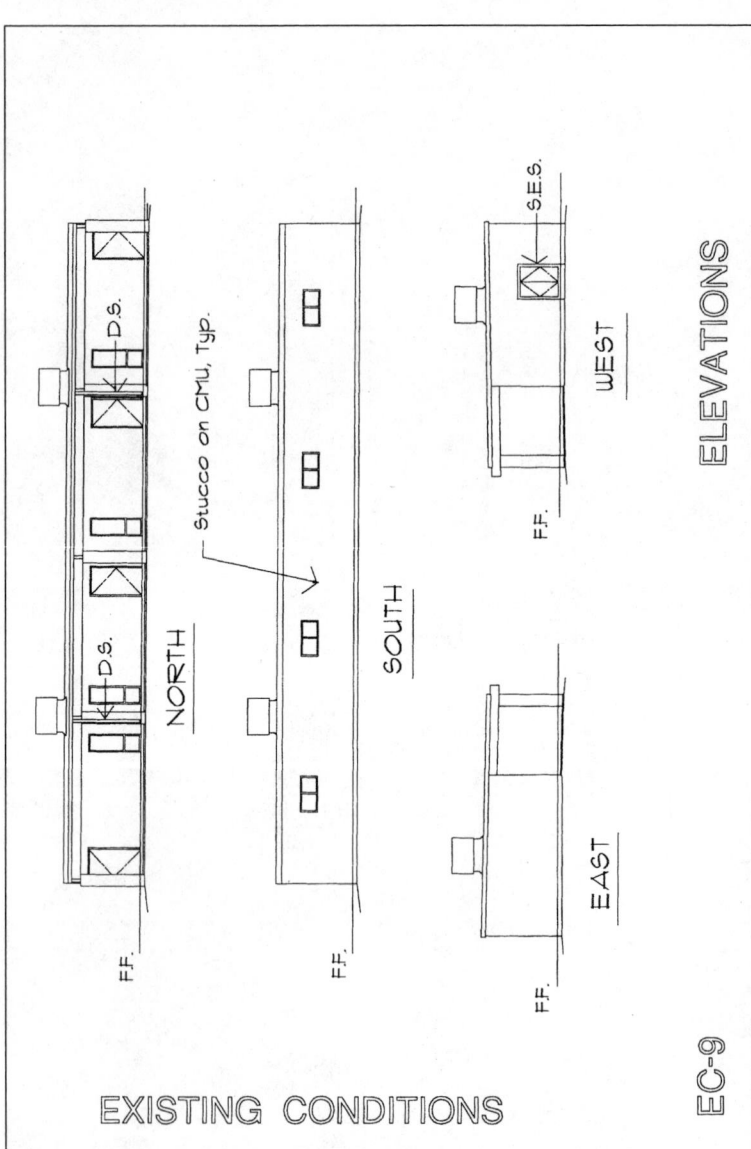

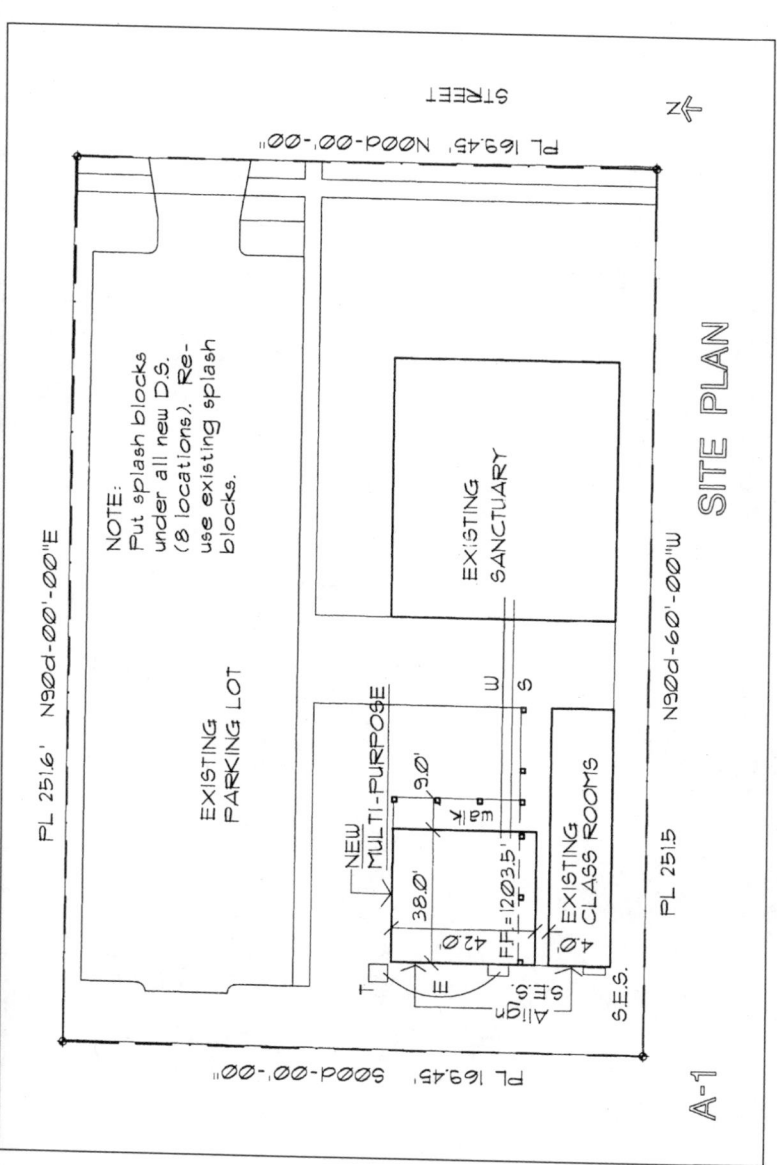

SITE PLAN

A-1

Exercise

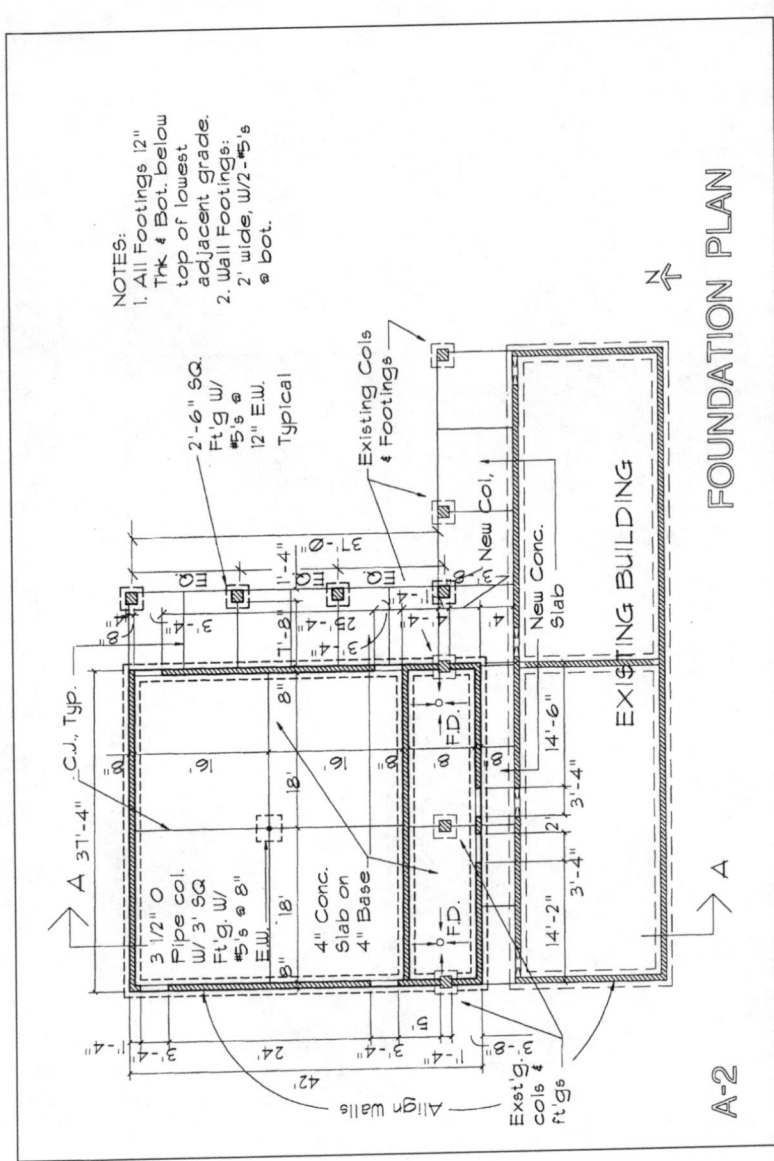

FOUNDATION PLAN

NOTES:
1. All Footings 12"
   Trk & Bot. below
   top of lowest
   adjacent grade.
2. Wall Footings:
   2' wide, w/2-#5's
   @ bot.

2'-6" SQ.
Ft'g w/
#5's @
12" E.W.
Typical

Existing Cols
& Footings

New Col.

New Conc.
Slab

EXISTING BUILDING

3 1/2" O
Pipe col.
w/3' SQ
Ft'g. w/
#5's @ 8"
E.W.

4" Conc.
Slab on
4" Base

C.J., Typ.

Align walls

Exist'g. cols &
ft'gs

A-2

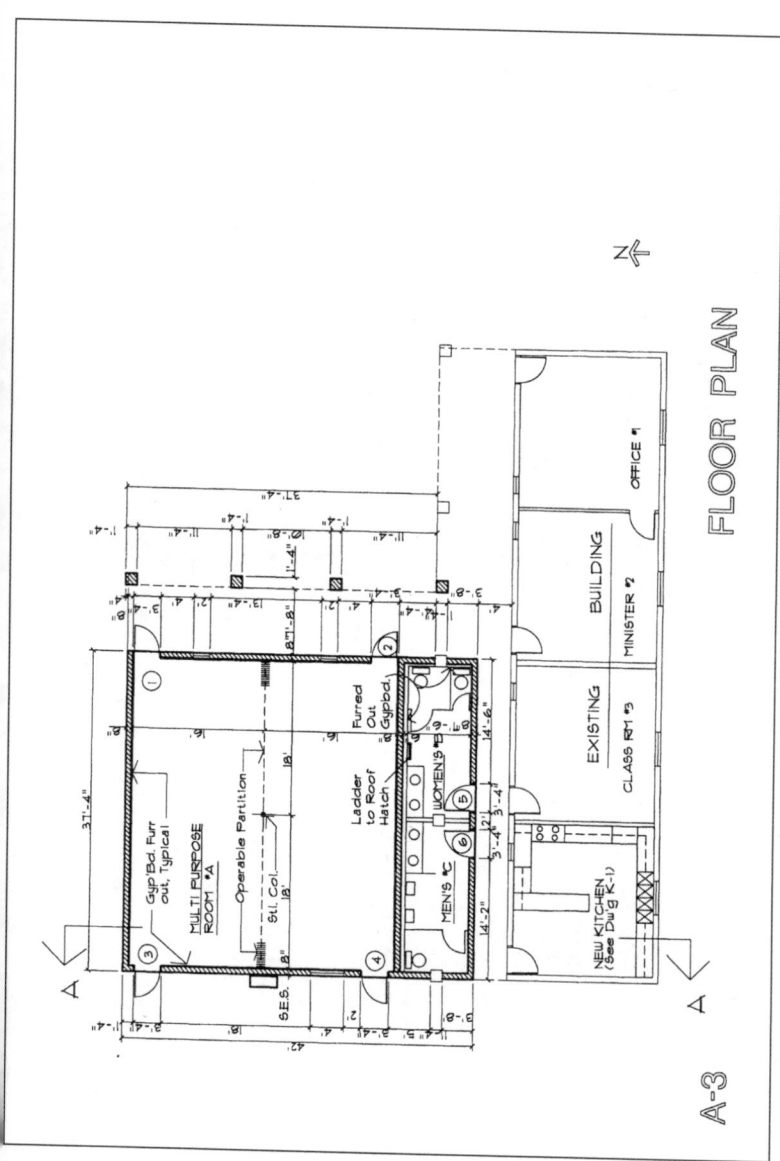

FLOOR PLAN

A-3

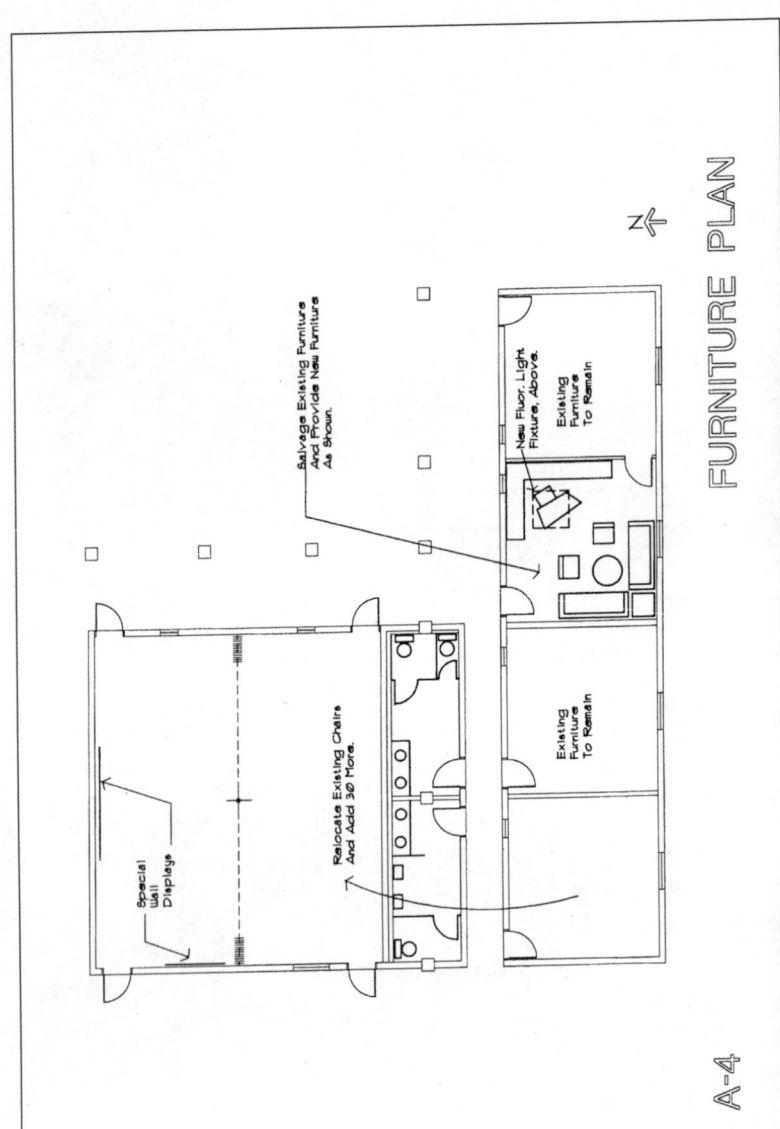

FURNITURE PLAN

Salvage Existing Furniture
And Provide New Furniture
As Shown.

New Fluor. Light
Fixture, Above.

Existing
Furniture
To Remain

Existing
Furniture
To Remain

Special
Wall
Displays

Relocate Existing Chairs
And Add 30 More.

N

A-4

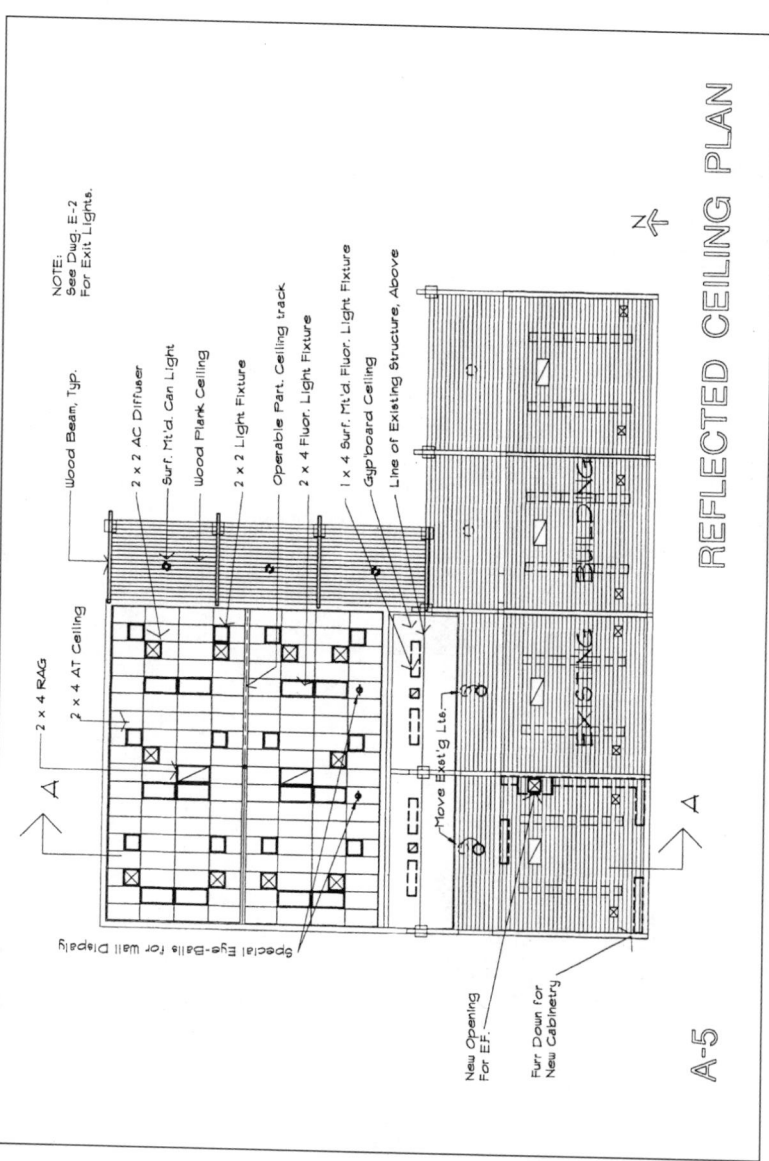

REFLECTED CEILING PLAN

NOTE:
See Dwg. E-2
For Exit Lights.

Wood Beam, Typ.
2 x 2 AC Diffuser
Surf. Mt'd. Can Light
Wood Plank Ceiling
2 x 2 Light Fixture
Operable Part. Ceiling track
2 x 4 Fluor. Light Fixture
1 x 4 Surf. Mt'd. Fluor. Light Fixtures
Gyp'board Ceiling
Line of Existing Structure, Above

2 x 4 AT Ceiling
2 x 4 RAG

Special Eye-Balls for Wall Display

Move Exist'g. Lts.

New Opening
For E.F.

Furr Down for
New Cabinetry

EXISTING   BUILDING

A-5

A

A

Exercise

115

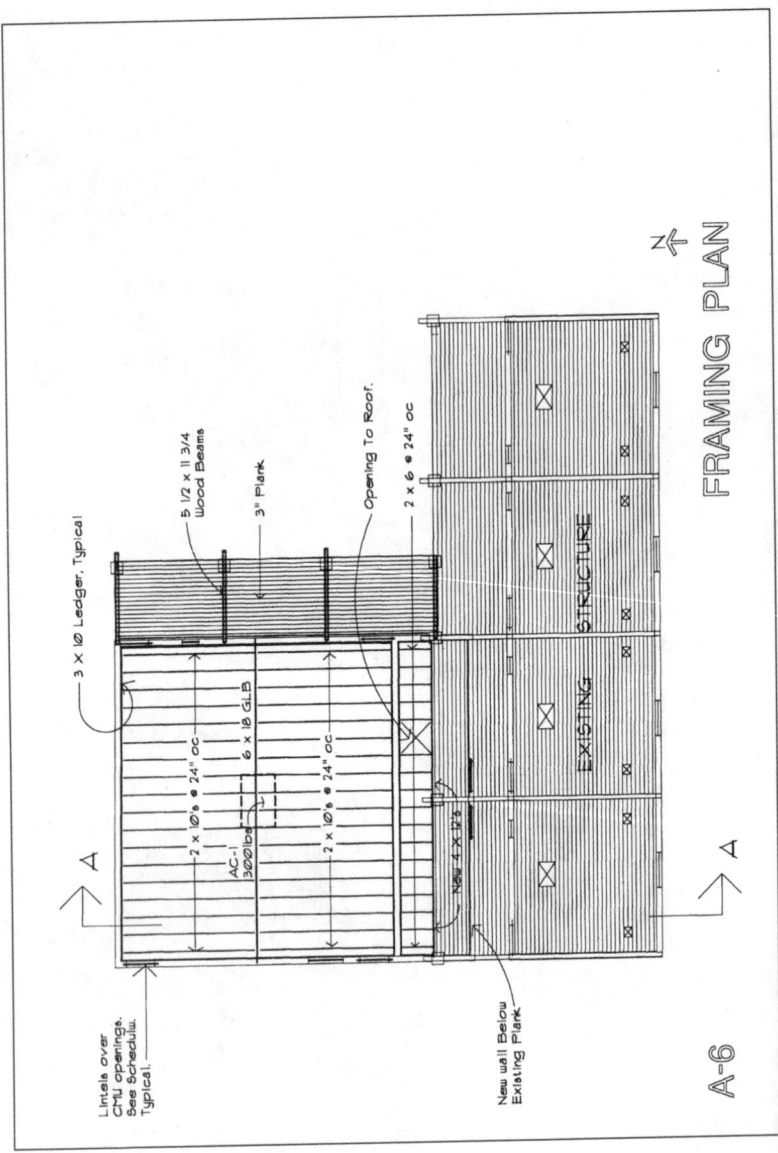

Lintels over CHU openings. See Schedule. Typical.

3 × 10 Ledger, Typical

5 1/2 × 11 3/4 Wood Beams

3" Plank

Opening To Roof.

2 × 6 @ 24" oc

2 × 10 @ 24" oc

6 × 10 GLB

AC-1 3200 lbs

2 × 10 @ 24" oc

New wall Below Existing Plank

New 4 × 12's

EXISTING STRUCTURE

FRAMING PLAN

A-6

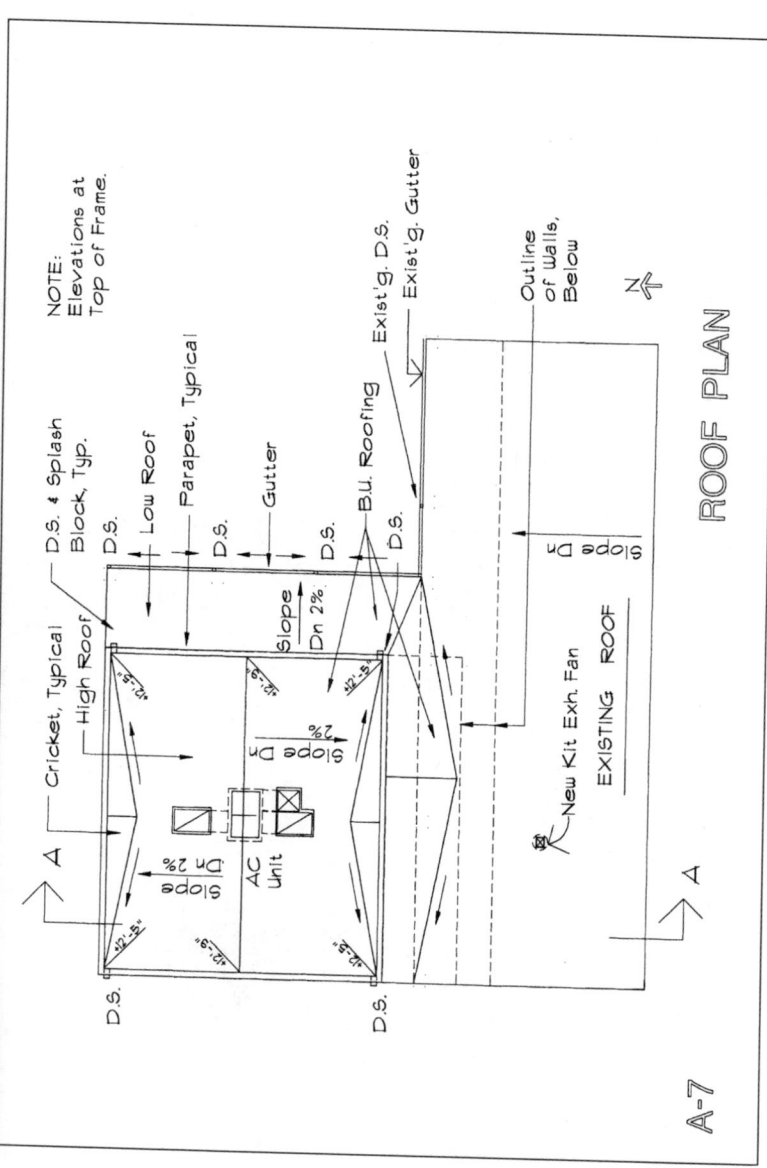

NOTE:
Elevations at
Top of Frame.

D.S. & Splash
Block, Typ.

Cricket, Typical

High Roof

D.S.

Low Roof

Parapet, Typical

D.S.

Gutter

D.S.

B.U. Roofing

Exist'g. D.S.

Exist'g. Gutter

D.S.

Slope
Dn 2%

Slope
Dn 2%

AC
Unit

D.S.

D.S.

New Kit Exh Fan

EXISTING ROOF

Outline
of Walls,
Below

Slope Dn

N

ROOF PLAN

A-7

ROOM FINISH SCHEDULE

NOTES:
1. Paint on Gyp Board.
2. Paint on Block.

ROOM NO.	ROOM NAME	FLOOR Vinyl	FLOOR Carpet	BASE Vinyl	WALLS North	WALLS South	WALLS East	WALLS West	CEILING Gypboard	CEILING A.T.	CEILING Gypboard	CEILING HEIGHT	NOTES
	NEW BUILDING												
A	Multi-Purpose Rm.	X		X	1	1	1	1		X		8'-0"	New
B	Women's Room	X		X									New
C	Toilet	X		X									New
	EXISTING BUILDING												
1	Office												Existing, No Changes
2	Minister		X	X	2	2							Remodel
3	Class Room				2	2							Existing, No Change
4	Kitchen	X		X	2	2	1	2					Remodel Existing Class Room

DOOR SCHEDULE

NO.	DOOR TYPE	WIDTH-HEIGHT	THK.	MATL.	FINISH	FRAME MATL.	FRAME FINISH	FRAME DET.	HARD.	NOTES
										NEW BUILDING
1	A	3'-0" 7'-0"	1 3/4"	Wd/SC		Metal	Paint	Paint		
2	B			H.M.						
3	B									
4	A			Wd/SC						
5	A									
6										EXISTING BUILDING
A										
B										
C										
D										
E										

SCHEDULES

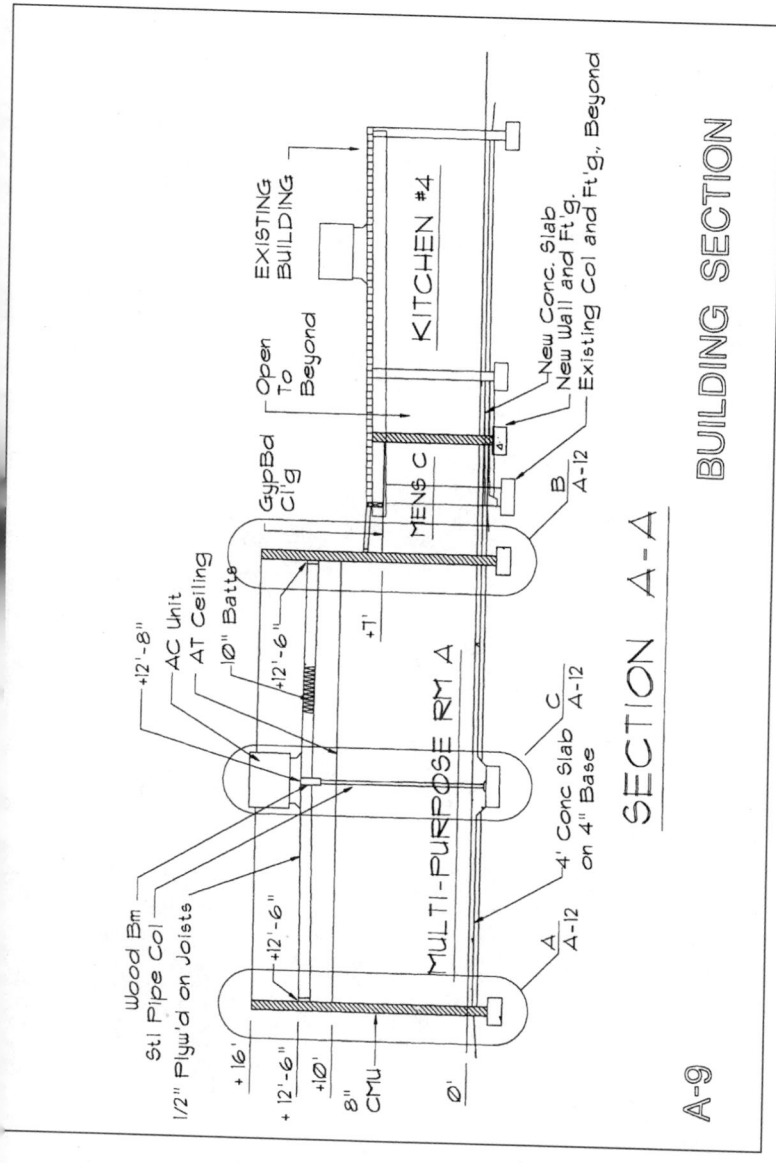

SECTION A-A

BUILDING SECTION

A-9

Exercise

119

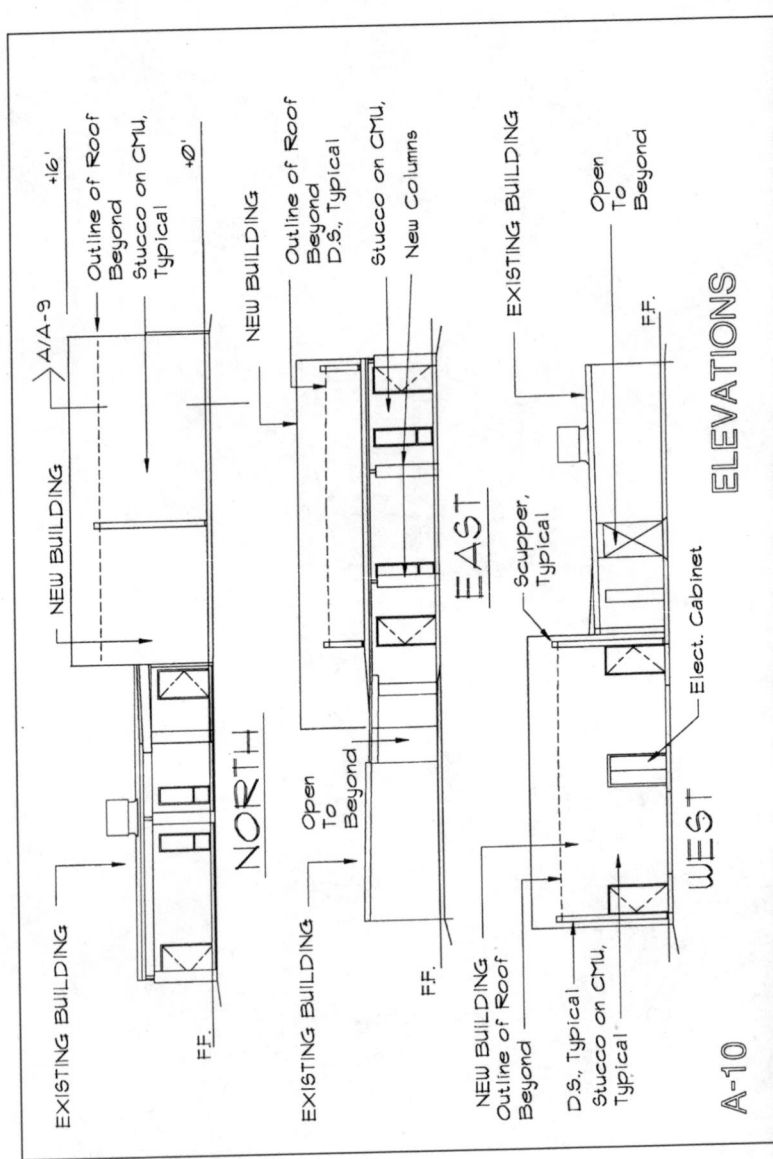

EXISTING BUILDING

NEW BUILDING

A/A-9

Outline of Roof Beyond

Stucco on CMU, Typical

+16'

+0'

FF.

NORTH

NEW BUILDING

EXISTING BUILDING

Outline of Roof Beyond D.S., Typical

Stucco on CMU, Typical

New Columns

Open To Beyond

FF.

EAST

Scupper, Typical

EXISTING BUILDING

Open To Beyond

FF.

Elect. Cabinet

NEW BUILDING Outline of Roof Beyond

D.S., Typical Stucco on CMU, Typical

WEST

ELEVATIONS

A-10

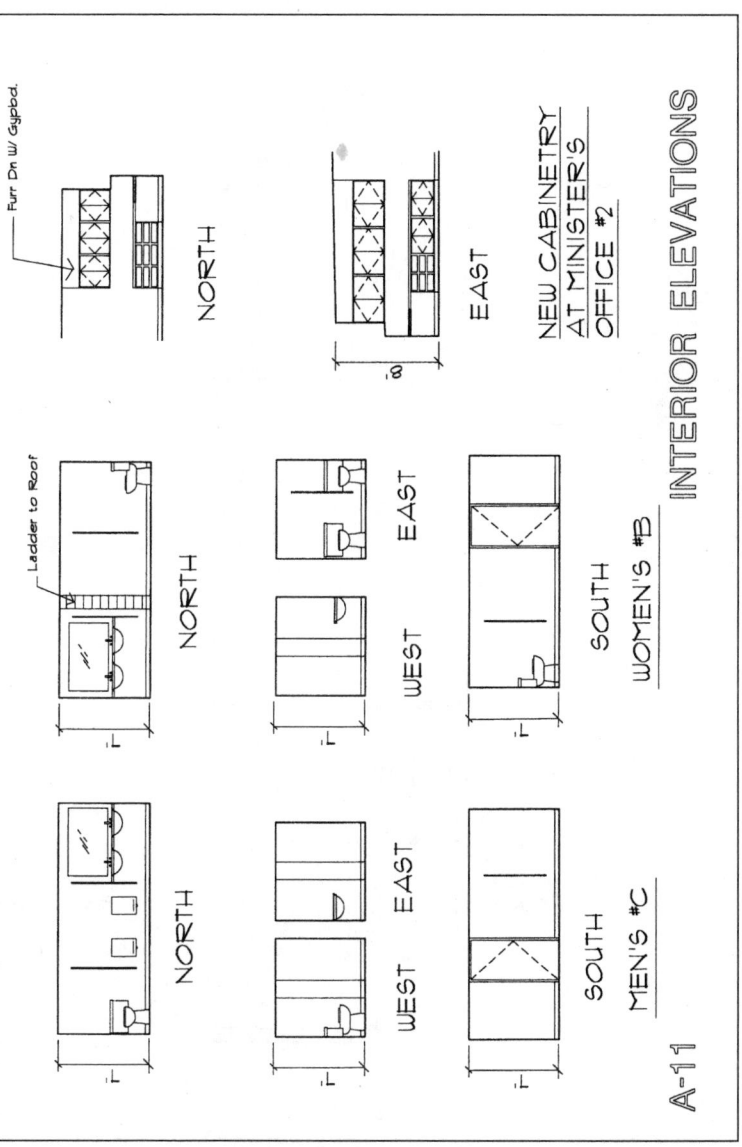

Furr Dn W/ Gypbd.

NORTH

EAST

NEW CABINETRY
AT MINISTER'S
OFFICE #2

Ladder to Roof

NORTH

NORTH

EAST

WEST

WEST

EAST

SOUTH

SOUTH

WOMEN'S #B

MEN'S #C

INTERIOR ELEVATIONS

A-11

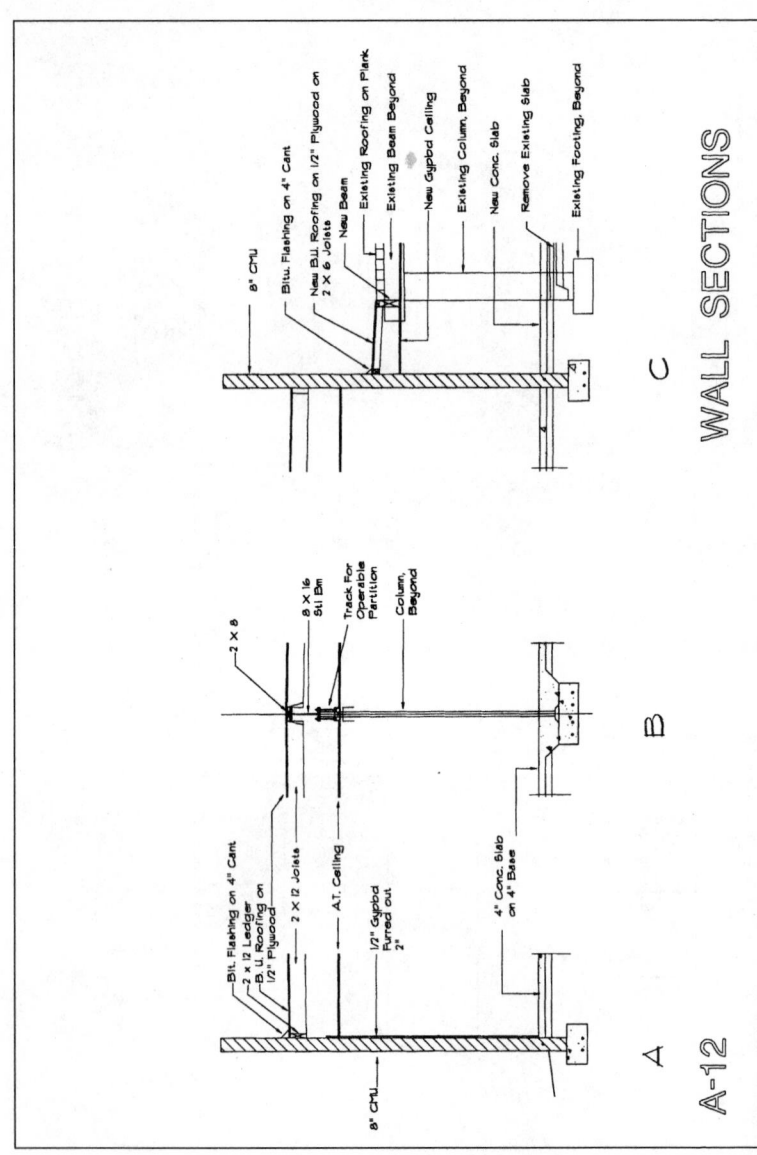

8" CMU

Btu. Flashing on 4" Cant.

New B.U. Roofing on 1/2" Plywood on
2 X 6 Joists

Existing Roofing on Plank

New Beam

Existing Beam Beyond

New Gypbd Ceiling

Existing Column, Beyond

New Conc. Slab

Remove Existing Slab

Existing Footing, Beyond

C

WALL SECTIONS

2 X 8

8 X 16 S-1 Bm

Track For Operable Partition

Column, Beyond

Btl. Flashing on 4" Cant.

2 x 12 Ledger

B. U. Roofing on 1/2" Plywood

2 X 12 Joists

A.T. Ceiling

1/2" Gypbd Furred out 2"

4" Conc. Slab on 4" Base

8" CMU

A

B

A-12

Chapter Five

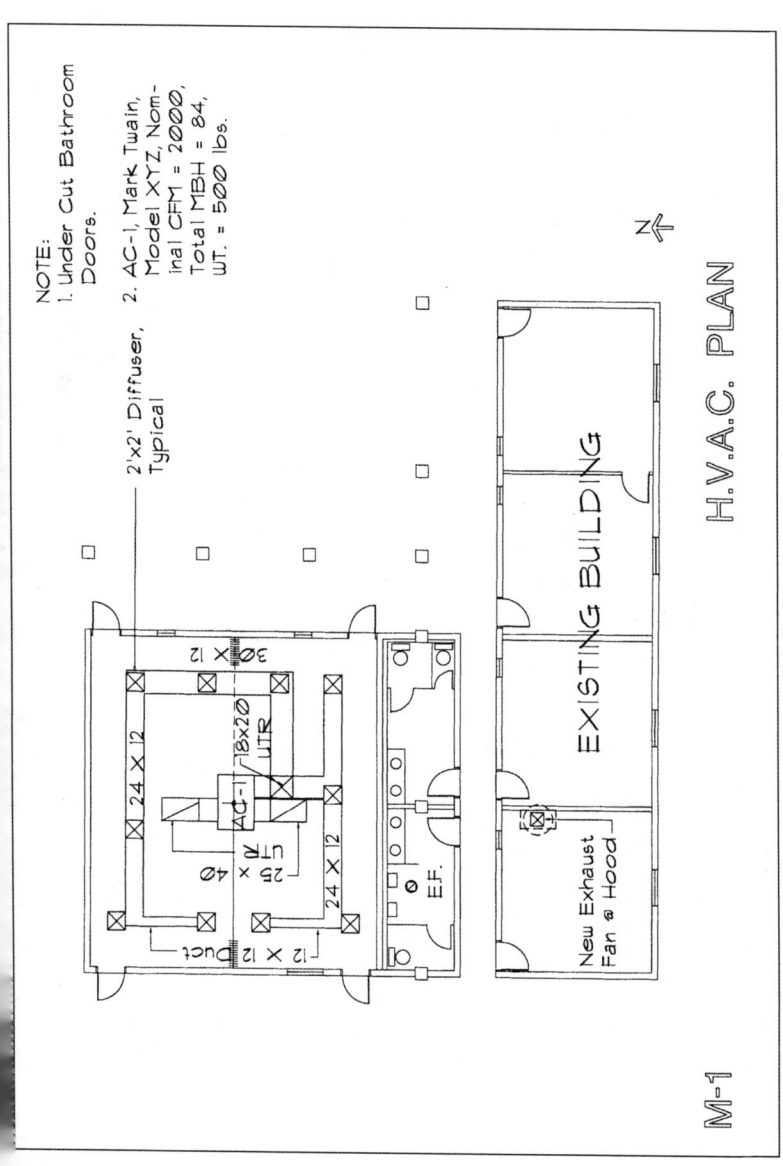

NOTE:
1. Under Cut Bathroom Doors.

2. AC-1, Mark Twain, Model XYZ, Nominal CFM = 2000, Total MBH = 84, WT. = 500 lbs.

2'x2' Diffuser, Typical

30 X 12

24 X 12

18x20 UTR

AC-1

25 X 40 UTR

24 X 12

12 X 12 Duct

E.F.

New Exhaust Fan @ Hood

EXISTING BUILDING

N

H.V.A.C. PLAN

M-1

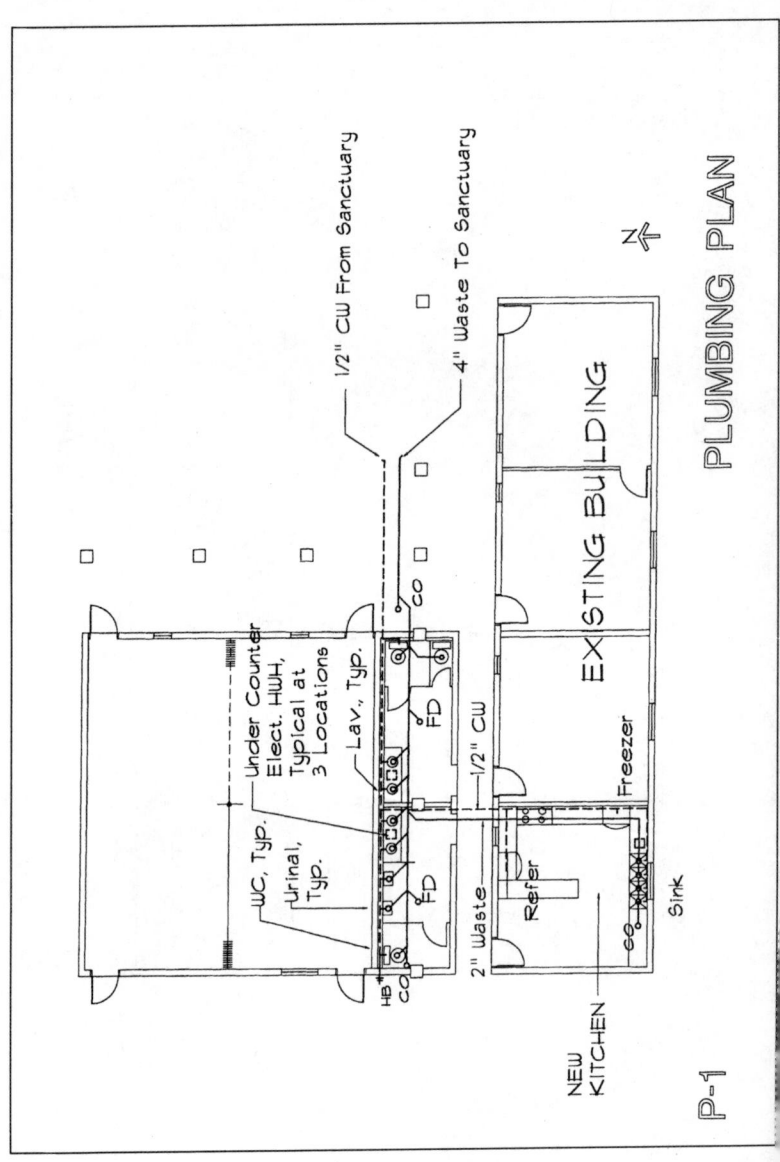

PLUMBING PLAN

1/2" CW From Sanctuary

4" Waste To Sanctuary

EXISTING BUILDING

N

Under Counter Elect. HWH, Typical at 3 Locations

Lav., Typ.

FD

1/2" CW

CO

WC, Typ.

Urinal, Typ.

FD

2" Waste

Refer

Freezer

HB

CO

NEW KITCHEN

CO

Sink

P-1

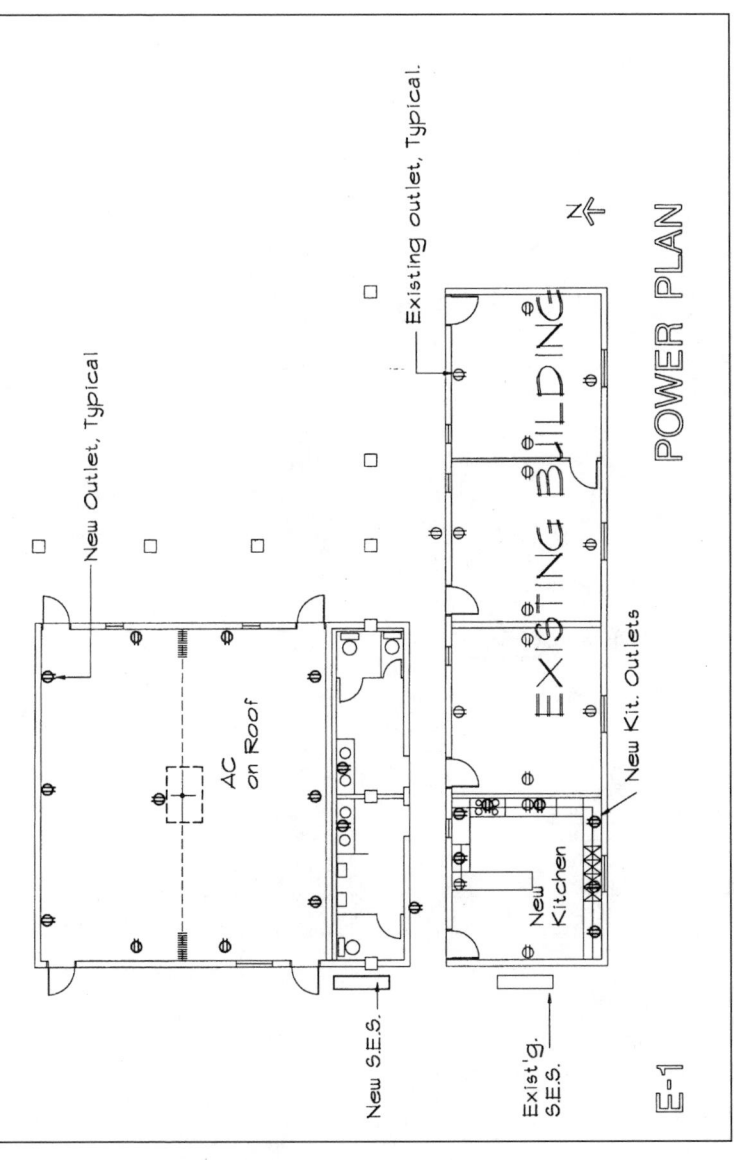

New Outlet, Typical

Existing outlet, Typical.

AC on Roof

New S.E.S.

Exist'g. S.E.S.

New Kitchen

New Kit. Outlets

N

EXISTING BUILDING

POWER PLAN

E-1

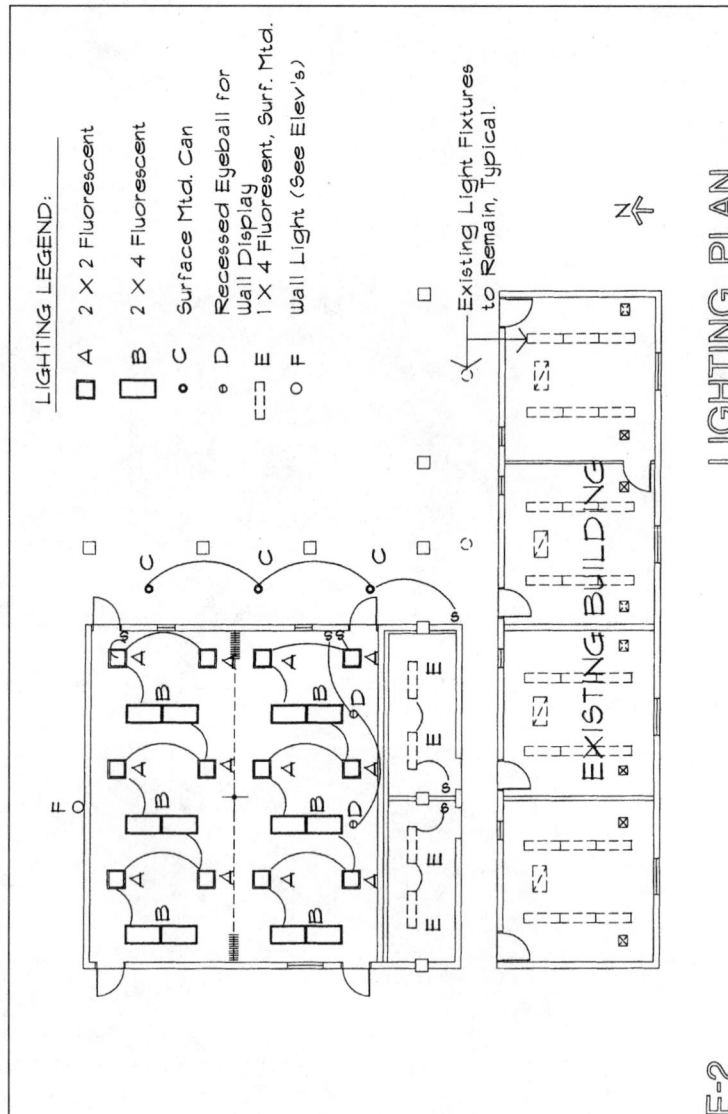

LIGHTING LEGEND:

☐ A   2 × 2 Fluorescent

☐ B   2 × 4 Fluorescent

• C   Surface Mtd. Can

⊕ D   Recessed Eyeball for
       Wall Display

⊏⊐ E 1 × 4 Fluorescent, Surf. Mtd.

○ F   Wall Light (See Elev's)

Existing Light Fixtures
to Remain, Typical.

N↗

EXISTING BUILDING

LIGHTING PLAN

E-2

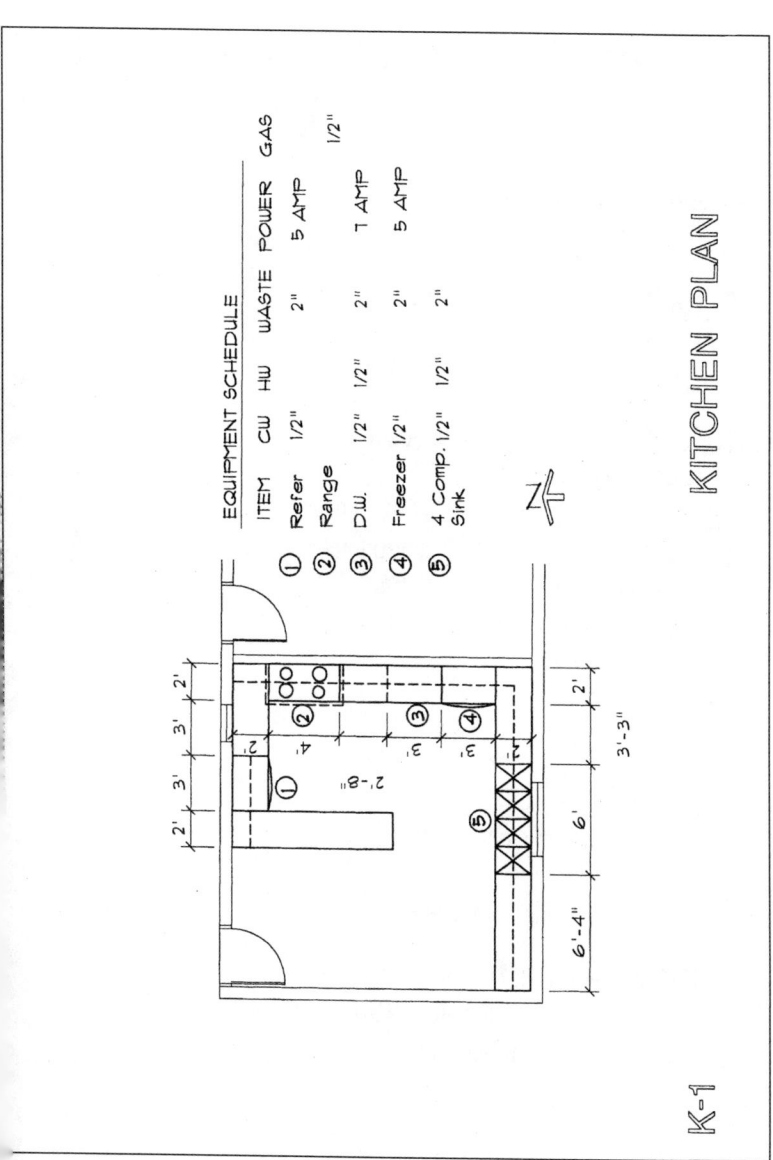

EQUIPMENT SCHEDULE

ITEM		CW	HW	WASTE	POWER	GAS
①	Refer	1/2"		2"	5 AMP	
②	Range					1/2"
③	D.W.	1/2"	1/2"	2"	7 AMP	
④	Freezer	1/2"		2"	5 AMP	
⑤	4 Comp. Sink	1/2"	1/2"	2"		

KITCHEN PLAN

K-1

Exercise

127

MULTIPURPOSE ROOM
ADDITION SPECIFICATIONS
TABLE OF CONTENTS

DIVISION 5—METALS

____ 05100 STRUCTURAL METALS

____ 05500 MISC. METALS

DIVISION 6—WOOD AND PLASTICS

____ 06100 ROUGH CARPENTRY

____ 06200 FINISH CARPENTRY

____ 06400 ARCHITECTURAL WOODWORK

____ 06600 PLASTIC FABRICATIONS

DIVISION 7—THERMAL AND MOISTURE PROTECTION

____ 07500 MEMBRANE ROOFING

____ 07600 FLASHING AND SHEET METAL

____ 07900 JOINT SEALERS

DIVISION 8—DOORS AND WINDOWS

____ 08050 BASIC DOOR AND WINDOW MATERIALS AND METHODS

____ 08100 METAL DOORS AND FRAMES

____ 08500 WINDOWS

____ 08700 HARDWARE

____ 08800 GLAZING

DIVISION 9—FINISHES

____ 09100 METAL SUPPORT ASSEMBLIES

____ 09200 PLASTER AND GYPSUM BOARD

____ 09300 TILE

____ 09400 TERRAZZO

____ 09500 CEILINGS

____ 09600 RESILIENT FLOORING,
       CARPET

____ 09900 PAINTING

DIVISION 10—SPECIALTIES

____ 10150 TOILET COMPARTMENTS

____ 10800 TOILET ACCESSORIES

DIVISION 11—EQUIPMENT

____ 11400   FOOD SERVICE EQUIPMENT

DIVISION 12—FURNISHINGS

____ 12100   ART

____ 12400   FURNISHINGS AND ACCESSORIES

____ 12500   FURNITURE

____ 12600   MULTIPLE SEATING

DIVISION 13—SPECIAL CONSTRUCTION

NOT USED

DIVISION 14—CONVEYING SYSTEMS

NOT USED

DIVISION 15—MECHANICAL

____ 15050   BASIC MECHANICAL MATERIALS AND METHODS

____ 15400   PLUMBING FIXTURES AND EQUIPMENT

____ 15700   HEATING, VENTILATING, AND AIR CONDITIONING

____ 15950   TESTING, ADJUSTING, AND BALANCING

DIVISION 16—ELECTRICAL

____ 16050   BASIC ELECTRICAL MATERIALS AND METHODS

____ 16200   ELECTRICAL POWER

____ 16500   LIGHTING

EXERCISE ANSWERS

The following pages 132 through 151 are redlines of Drawings A-1 through K-1, plus the Table of Contents of the Specifications for the exercise project.

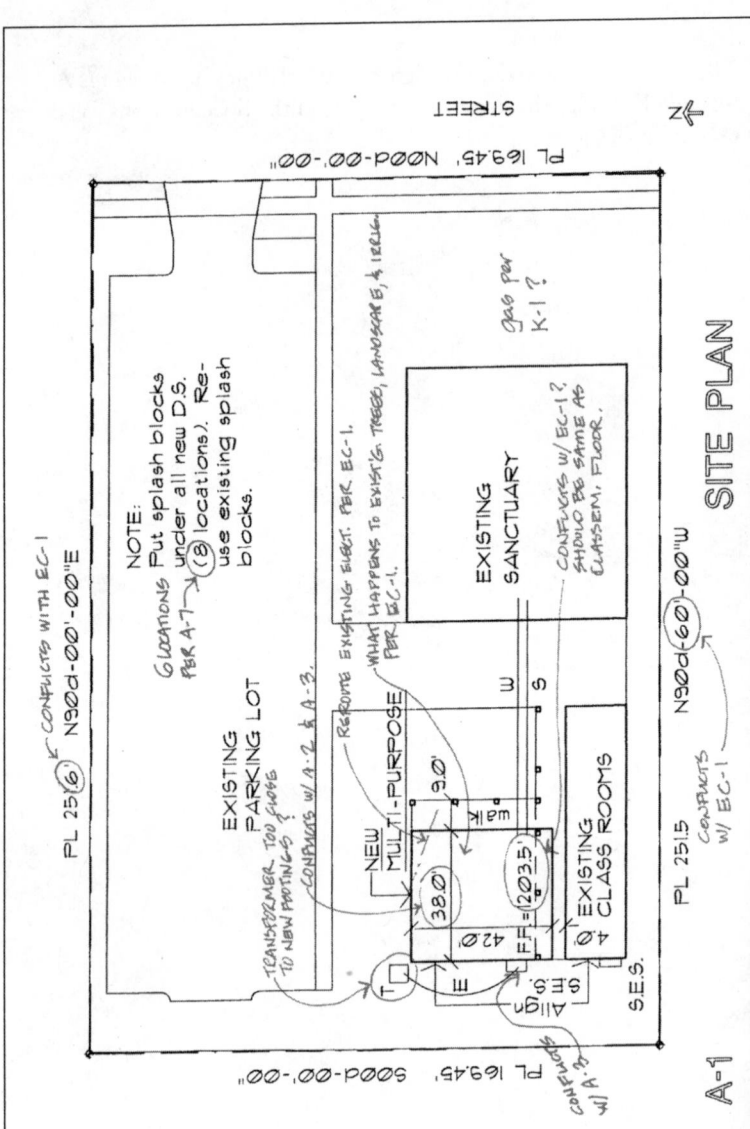

SITE PLAN

A-1

NOTE:
GIDEONONS Put splash blocks under all new D.S. (8 locations). Re-use existing splash blocks.

PER A-7

EXISTING PARKING LOT

PL 169.45'   N00d-00'-00"E

PL 25'.6"   N90d-00'-00"E ← CONFLICTS WITH EC-1

TRANSFORMER TOO CLOSE TO NEW PARTING? CONFLICTS W/ A-2 & A-3.

RE-ROUTE EXISTING SIDEWK. PER EC-1.

WHAT HAPPENS TO EXIST'G. TREES, LANDSCAPE & IRRIG. PER EC-1.

CONFLICTS W/ A-2 & A-3.

NEW MULTI-PURPOSE

walk

9.0'

38.0'

F.F.=(203.5')

42.0'

T

E

S.E.S.

Align

S.E.S.

4.0'

EXISTING CLASS ROOMS

CONFLICTS W/ A-3

W   S

EXISTING SANCTUARY

CONFLICTS W/ EC-1? SHOULD BE SAME AS CLASSRM. FLOOR.

Gas per K-1?

PL 251.5'   N90d-60'-00"W   CONFLICTS W/ EC-1

STREET

PL 169.45'   N00d-00'-00"E

N↙

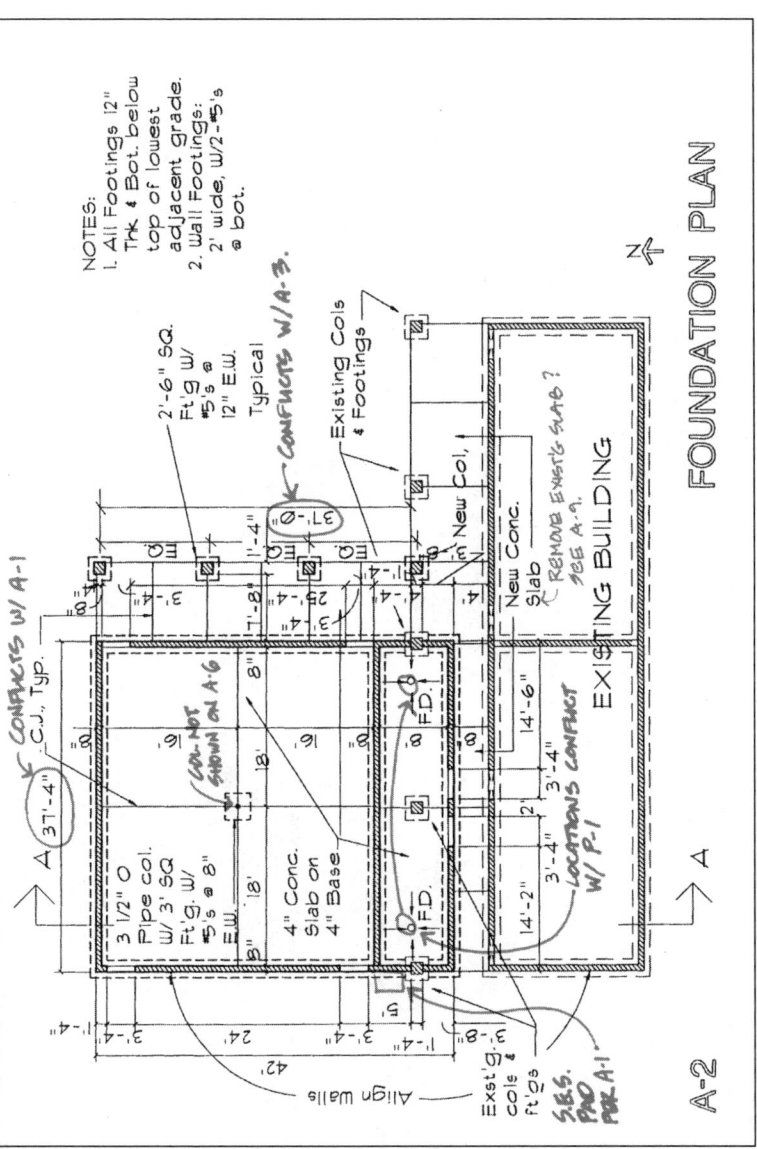

FOUNDATION PLAN

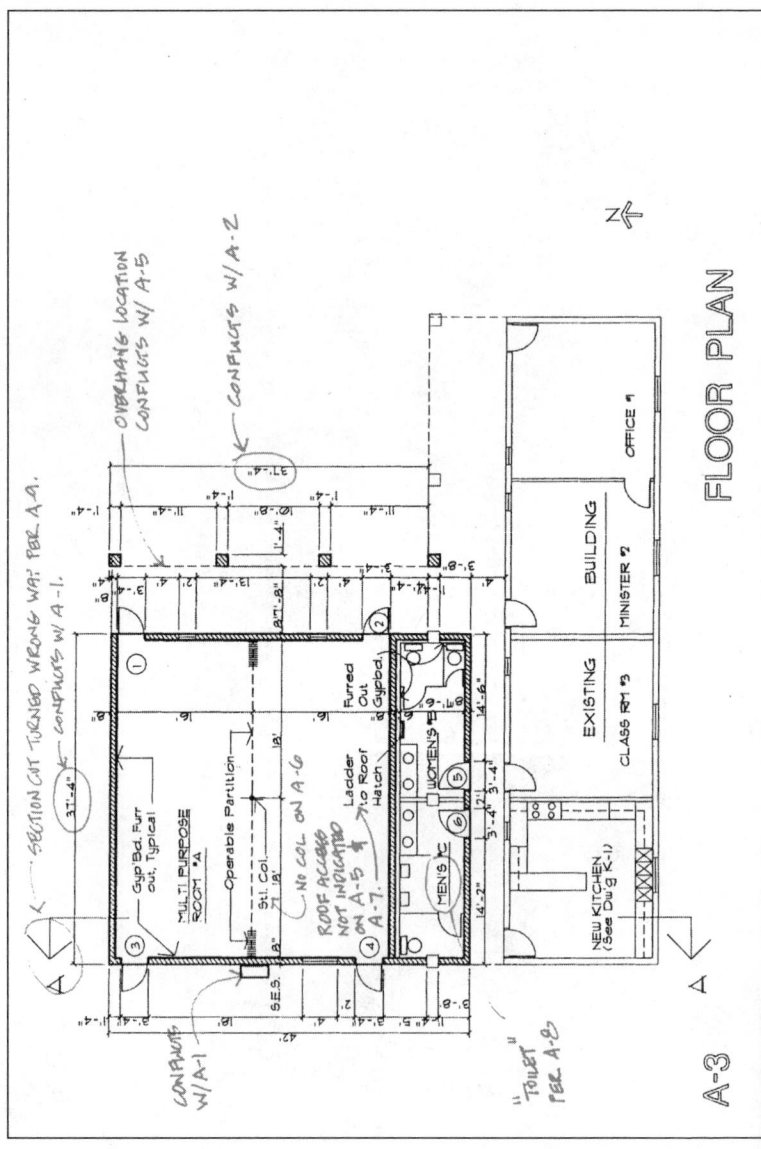

FLOOR PLAN

MULTI PURPOSE ROOM "A"

Gyp. Bd. Furr out, Typical

Operable Partition

St'l. Col.

Ladder to Roof Hatch

Furred Out Gyp. Bd.

WOMEN'S

MEN'S

EXISTING BUILDING

CLASS RM #3

MINISTER #2

OFFICE #1

NEW KITCHEN (See Dwg K-1)

"SECTION CUT TURNED WRONG WAY" PER A-4.

"CONFLICTS W/ A-1.

OVERHANG LOCATION CONFLICTS W/ A-5

CONFLICTS W/ A-2

"No COL ON A-6

ROOF ACCESS NOT INDICATED ON A-5 & A-7.

CONFLICTS W/ A-1

"TOILET" PER A-8

A-3

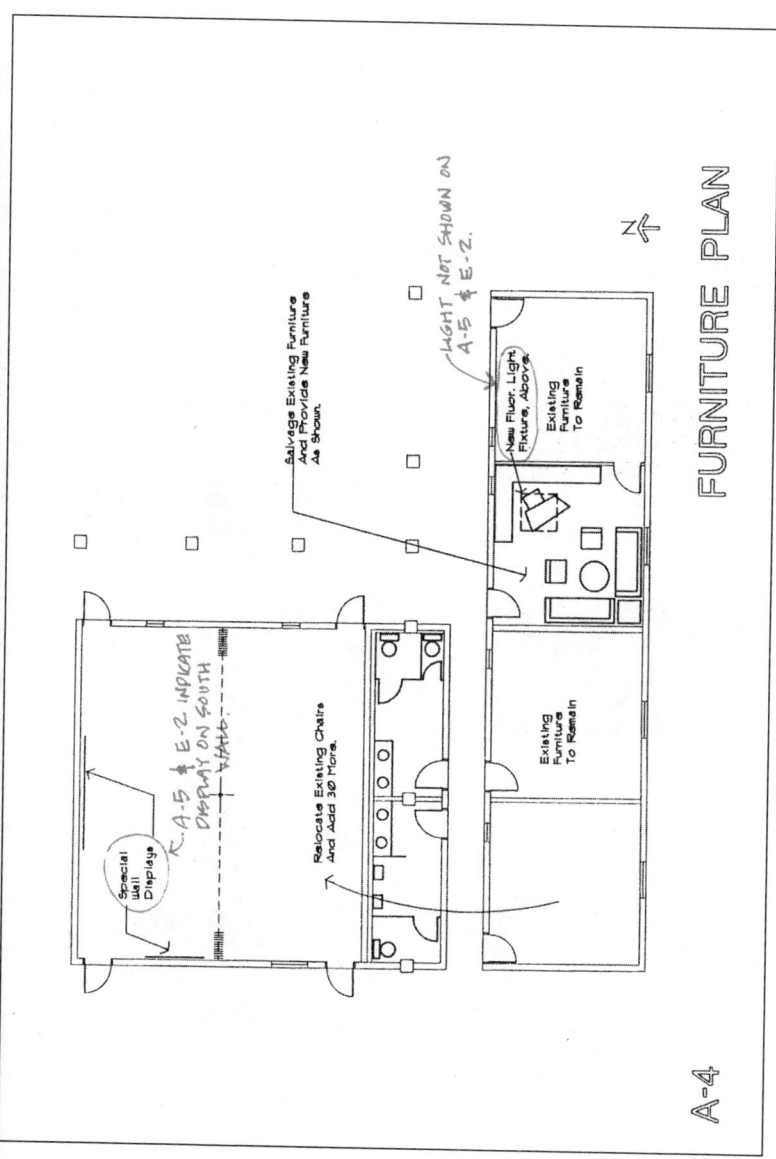

FURNITURE PLAN

Special
Wall
Displays

R.A.5 ¢ E-2. INDICATE
DISPLAY ON SOUTH
WALL.

Salvage Existing Furniture
And Provide New Furniture
As Shown.

LIGHT NOT SHOWN ON
A-5 ¢ E-2.

New Fluor. Light
Fixture, Above.

Existing
Furniture
To Remain

Relocate Existing Chairs
And Add 30 More.

Existing
Furniture
To Remain

N

A-4

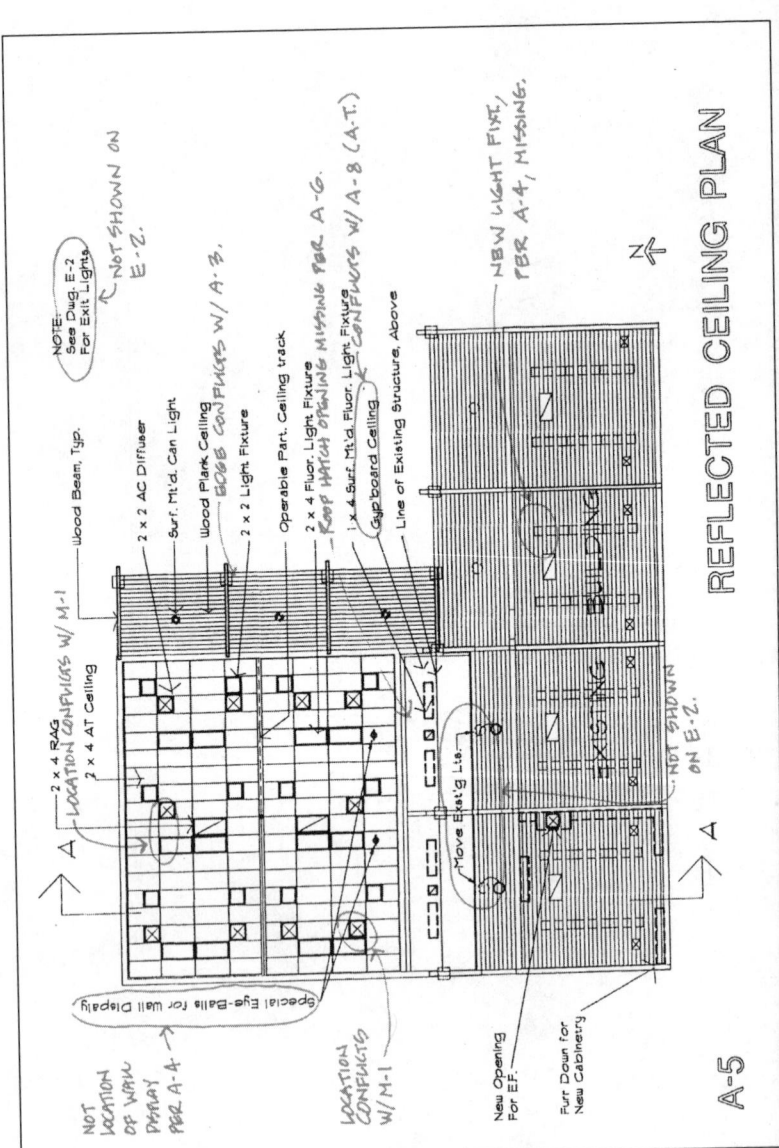

REFLECTED CEILING PLAN

A-5

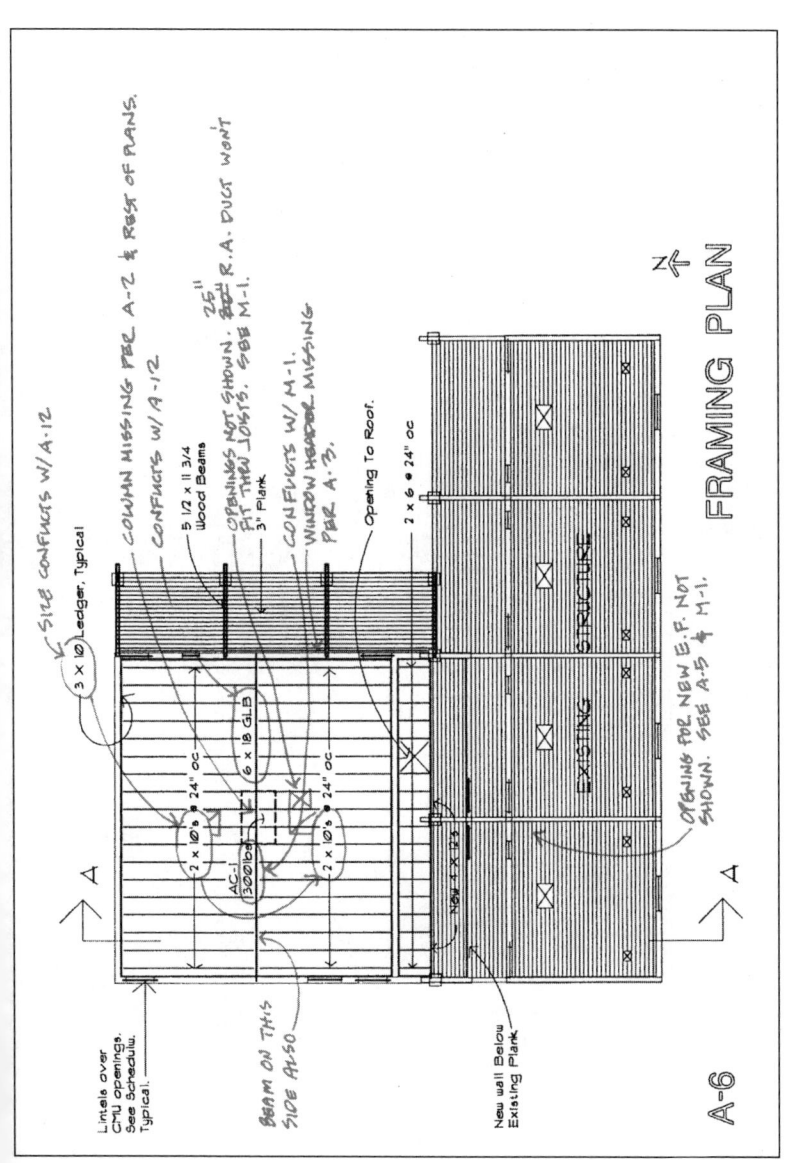

Limits over
CMU openings.
See Schedule.
Typical.

SIZE CONFLICTS W/ A-12

3 x 10 Ledger, Typical

COLUMN MISSING PER A-7 & REST OF PLANS.

CONFLICTS W/ A-12

5 1/2 x 11 3/4
Wood Beams

25"

OPENINGS NOT SHOWN. SEE R.A. DUCT WON'T
FIT THRU JOISTS. SEE M-1.

3" Plank

CONFLICTS W/ M-1.
WINDOW HEADER MISSING
PER A-3.

Opening To Roof.

2 x 6 @ 24" oc

2 x 10's @ 24" oc

6 x 18 GLB

AC-1
300 lbs

2 x 10's @ 24" oc

BEAM ON THIS
SIDE ALSO

EXISTING   STRUCTURE

NEW 4 x 125

OPENING FOR NEW E.F. NOT
SHOWN. SEE A-5 & M-1.

New wall Below
Existing Plank

A-6

A

A

FRAMING PLAN

N

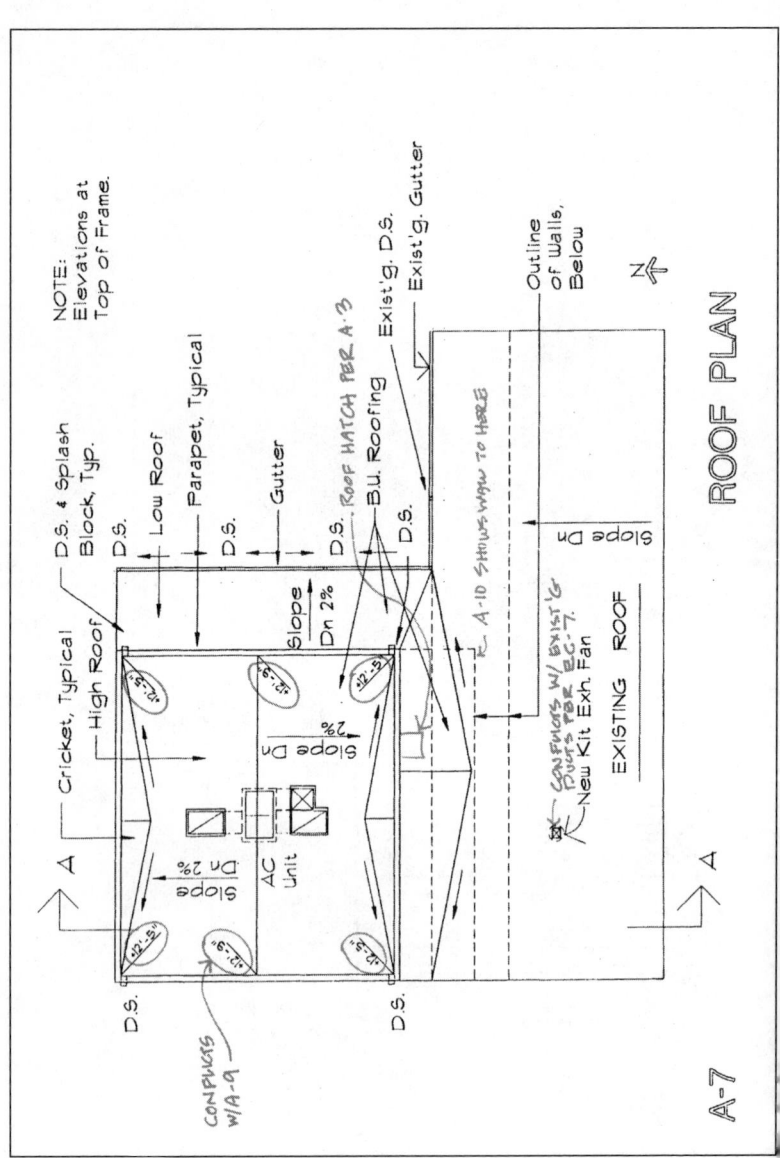

NOTE:
Elevations at
Top of Frame.

D.S. & Splash
Block, Typ.

Parapet, Typical

D.S.

Low Roof

Gutter

D.S.

Cricket, Typical

D.S. ROOF HATCH PER A-3

B.U. Roofing

Exist'g. D.S.

High Roof

D.S.

Exist'g. Gutter

A-10 SHOWS HOW TO HERE

Outline
of Walls,
Below

N

Slope
Dn 2%

2%
slope Dn

AC
Unit

slope
Dn 2%

CONFIRMS W/ EXIST'G
DUCTS FOR EC-7.
New Kit Exh Fan

slope Dn

EXISTING ROOF

D.S.

CONFIRMS
W/A-9

D.S.

ROOF PLAN

A-7

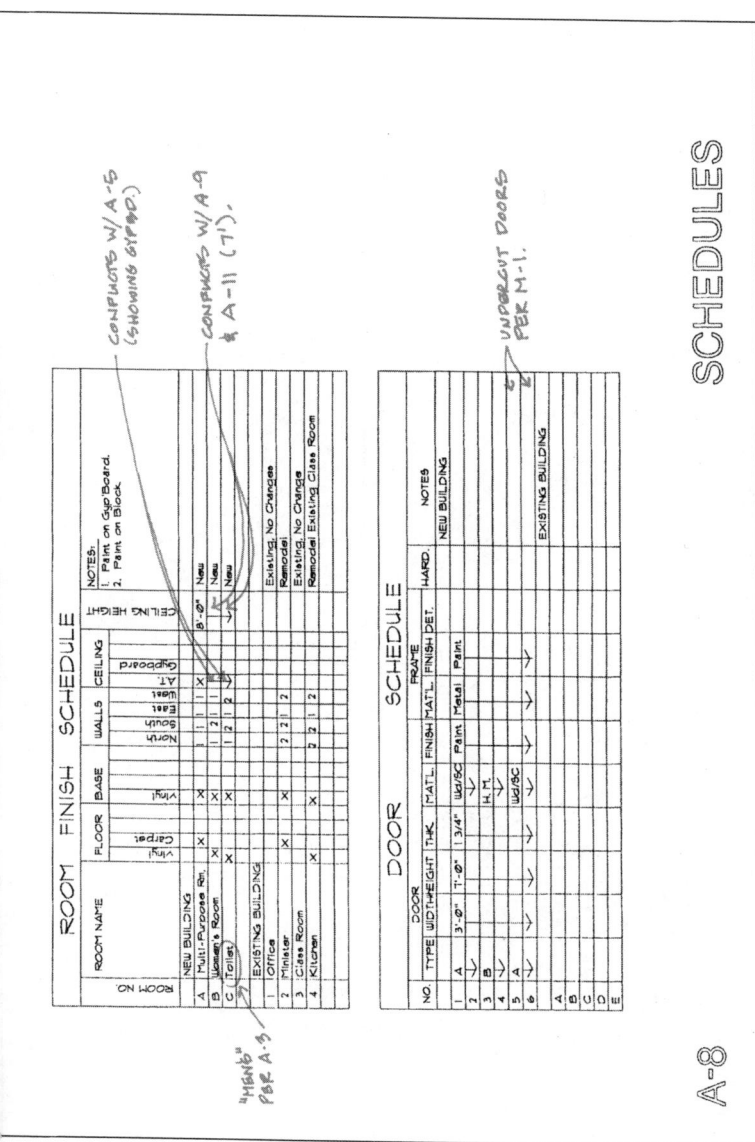

SCHEDULES

A-8

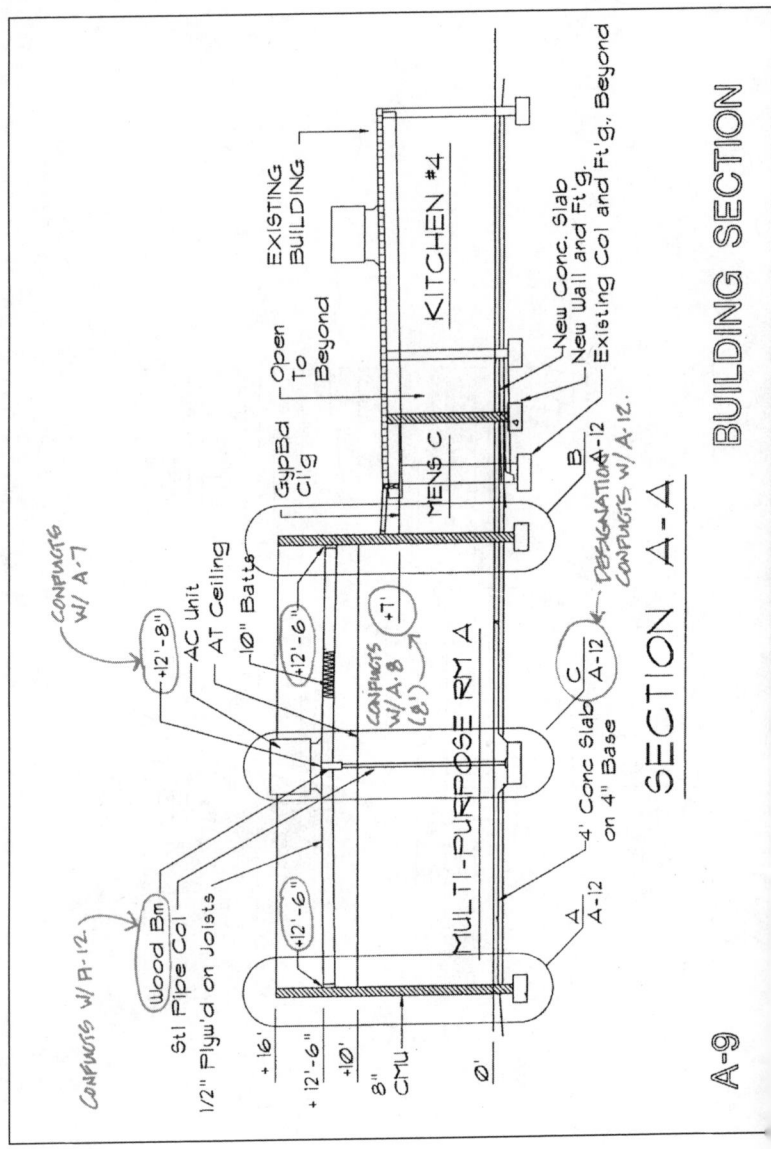

BUILDING SECTION

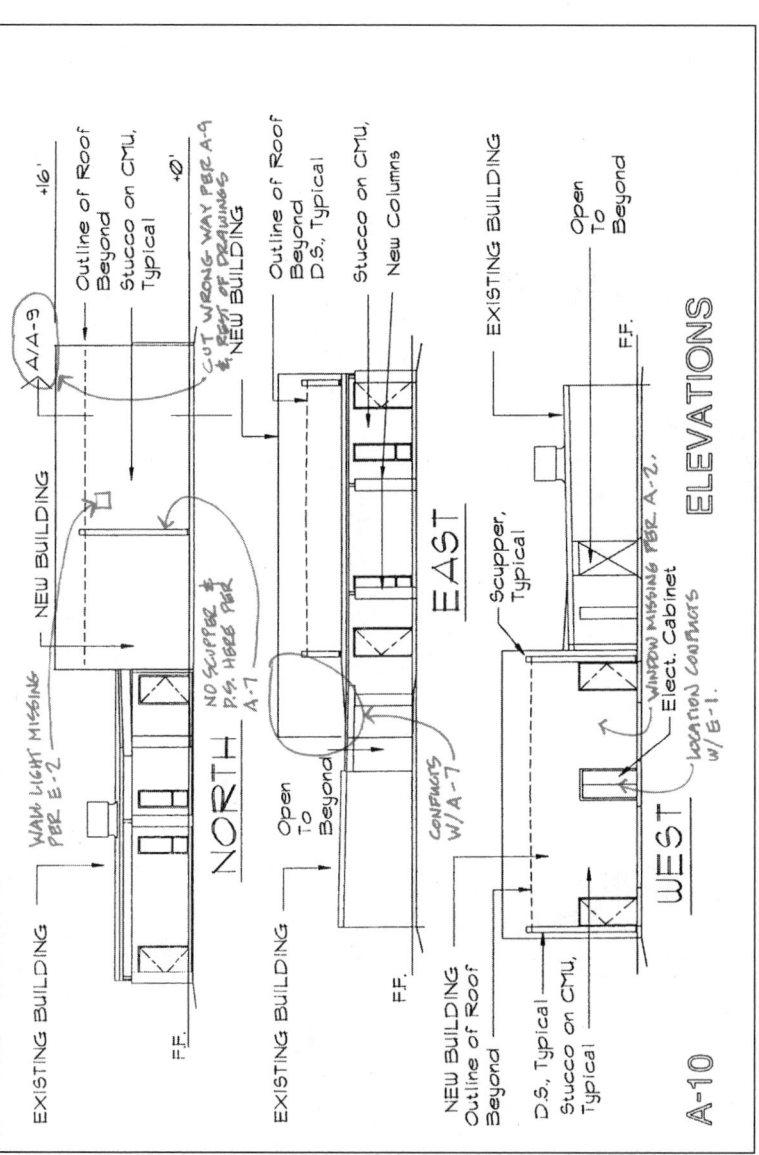

EXISTING BUILDING

WALL LIGHT MISSING PER E-2

NEW BUILDING

A/A-9

Outline of Roof Beyond

Stucco on CMU, Typical

CUT WRONG WAY PER A-9 & REST OF DRAWINGS

+16'

+0'

F.F.

NO SCUPPER & D.S. HERE PER A-7

NORTH

NEW BUILDING

EXISTING BUILDING

Open To Beyond

CONFLICTS W/A-7

F.F.

Outline of Roof Beyond D.S., Typical

Stucco on CMU,

New Columns

EAST

Scupper, Typical

NEW BUILDING Outline of Roof Beyond

D.S., Typical Stucco on CMU, Typical

EXISTING BUILDING

Open To Beyond

F.F.

Elect. Cabinet

WINDOW MISSING PER A-2, LOCATION CONFLICTS W/E-1.

WEST

ELEVATIONS

A-10

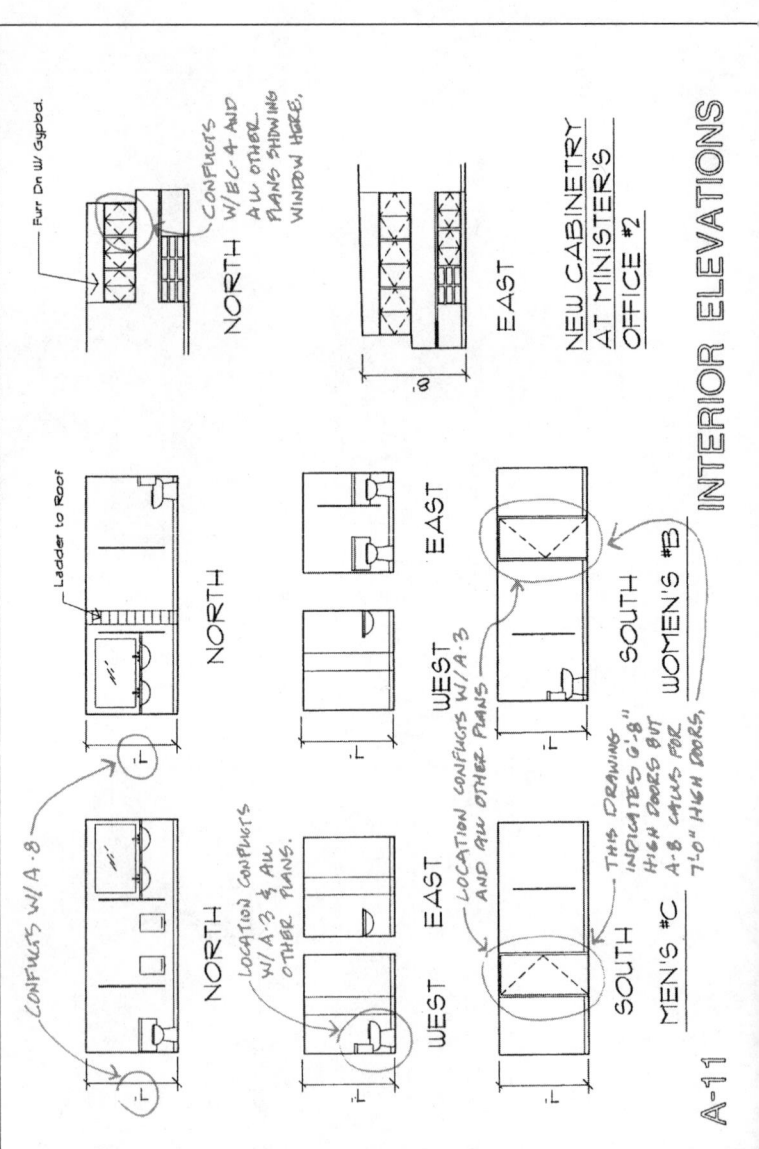

Furr Dn W/ Gypbd.

CONFLICTS
W/ EC-4 AND
ALL OTHER
PLANS SHOWING
WINDOW HERE.

NORTH

EAST

NEW CABINETRY
AT MINISTER'S
OFFICE #2

8'

Ladder to Roof

NORTH

EAST

CONFLICTS W/ A-8

CONFLICTS
W/ A-3 & ALL
OTHER PLANS.

NORTH   EAST

WEST

LOCATION CONFLICTS
W/ A-3 & ALL
OTHER PLANS.

LOCATION CONFLICTS W/ A-3
AND ALL OTHER PLANS.

WEST

SOUTH

WOMEN'S #B

THIS DRAWING
INDICATES 6'-8"
HIGH DOORS BUT
A-8 CALLS FOR
7'-0" HIGH DOORS.

SOUTH

MEN'S #C

A-11

INTERIOR ELEVATIONS

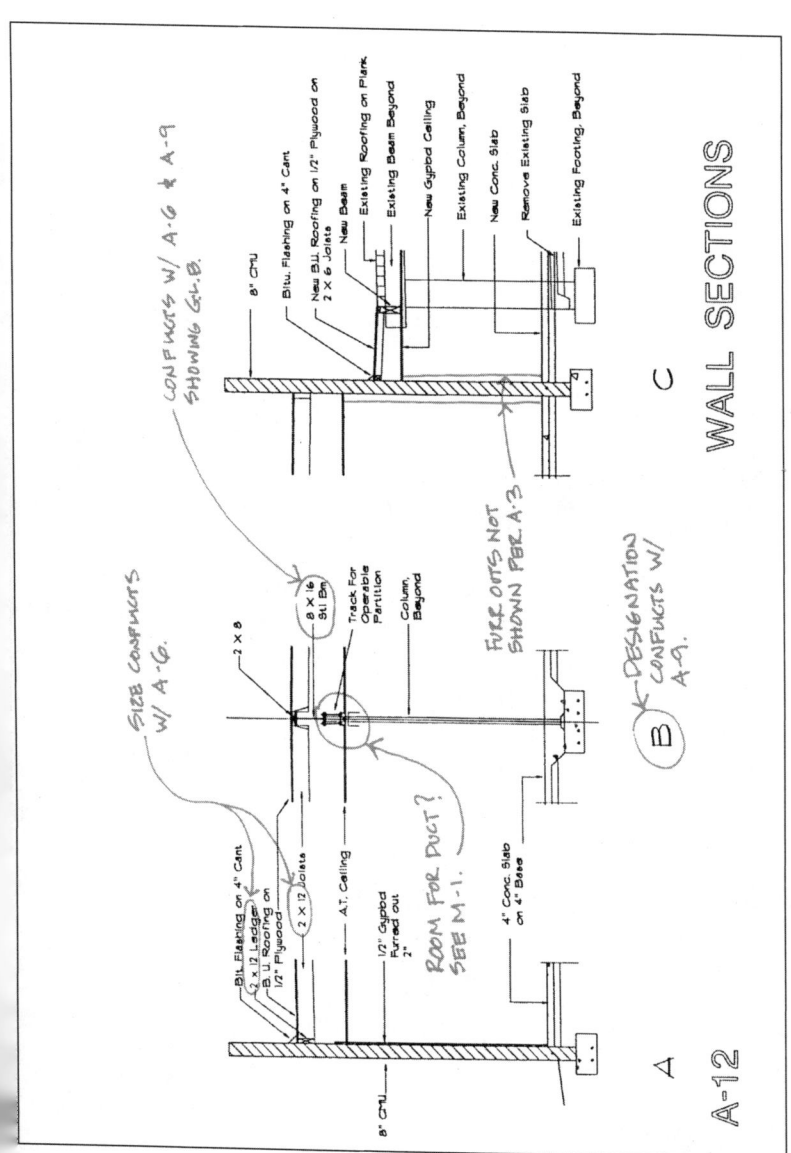

WALL SECTIONS

A-12

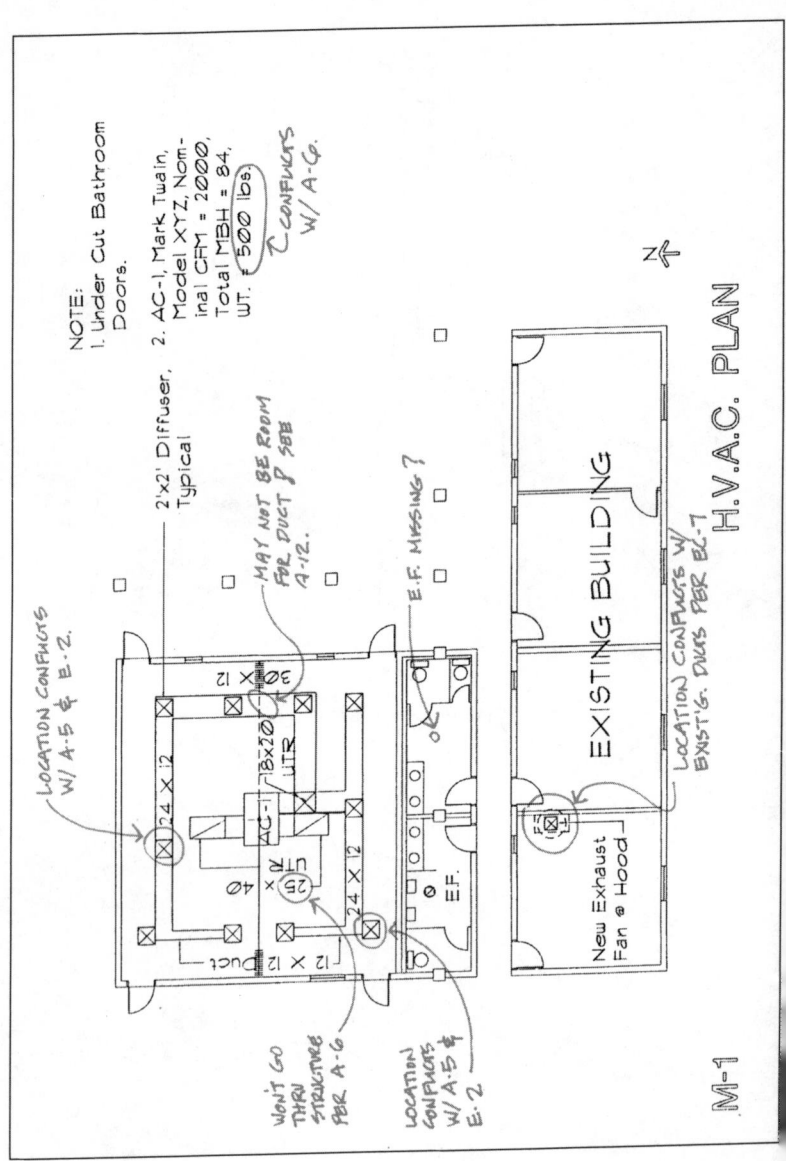

NOTE:
1. Under Cut Bathroom Doors.

2. AC-1, Mark Twain, Model XYZ, Nominal CFM = 2000, Total MBH = 84, WT. ≠ 500 lbs.

CONFLICTS W/ A-G.

2'x2' Diffuser, Typical

MAY NOT BE ROOM FOR DUCT ∮ SEE A-12.

E.F. MISSING ?

LOCATION CONFLICTS W/ A-5 ¢ E-2.

30 x 12

24 x 12

18x20 UTR

AC-1

40 x 40

UTR

26 x 24

24 x 12

12 x 12

Duct

WON'T GO THRU STRUCTURE PER A-6

LOCATION CONFLICTS W/ A-5 ¢ E-2

E.F.

New Exhaust Fan @ Hood

EXISTING BUILDING

LOCATION CONFLICTS W/ EXIST'G. DUCTS PER EL-7

H.V.A.C. PLAN

N↗

M-1

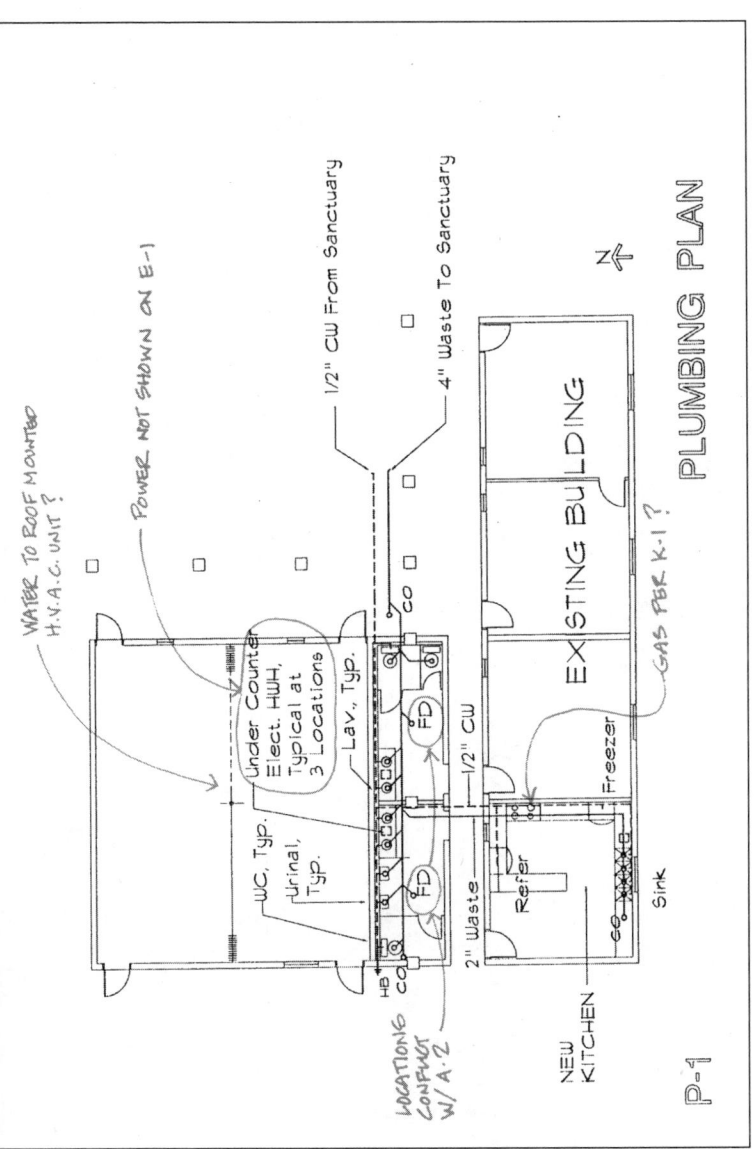

PLUMBING PLAN

WATER TO ROOF MOUNTED
H.V.A.C. UNIT ?

POWER NOT SHOWN ON E-1

1/2" CW From Sanctuary

4" Waste To Sanctuary

Under Counter
Elect. HWH,
Typical at
3 Locations

Lav., Typ.

WC, Typ.

Urinal, Typ.

FD

FD

CO

CO

1/2" CW

2" Waste

HB

CO

LOCATIONS
CONFIRM
W/ A-2

EXISTING BUILDING

NEW KITCHEN

Refer

Freezer

Sink

CO

GAS FOR K-1 ?

N

P-1

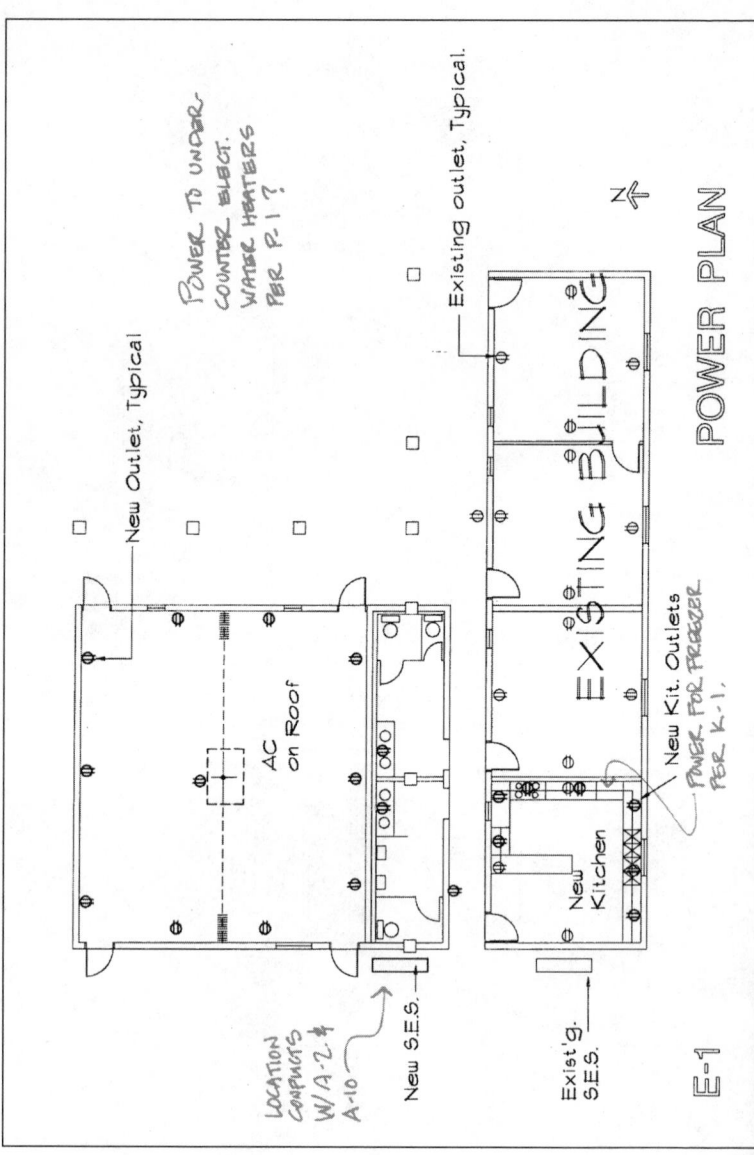

POWER PLAN

EXISTING BUILDING

New Outlet, Typical

Existing outlet, Typical.

POWER TO UNDER
COUNTER ELECT.
WATER HEATERS
PER P.1 ?

AC on Roof

New Kit. Outlets

POWER FOR FREEZER
PER K-1.

New Kitchen

LOCATION
CONDUIT'S
W/A-2 &
A-10

New S.E.S.

Exist'g. S.E.S.

E-1

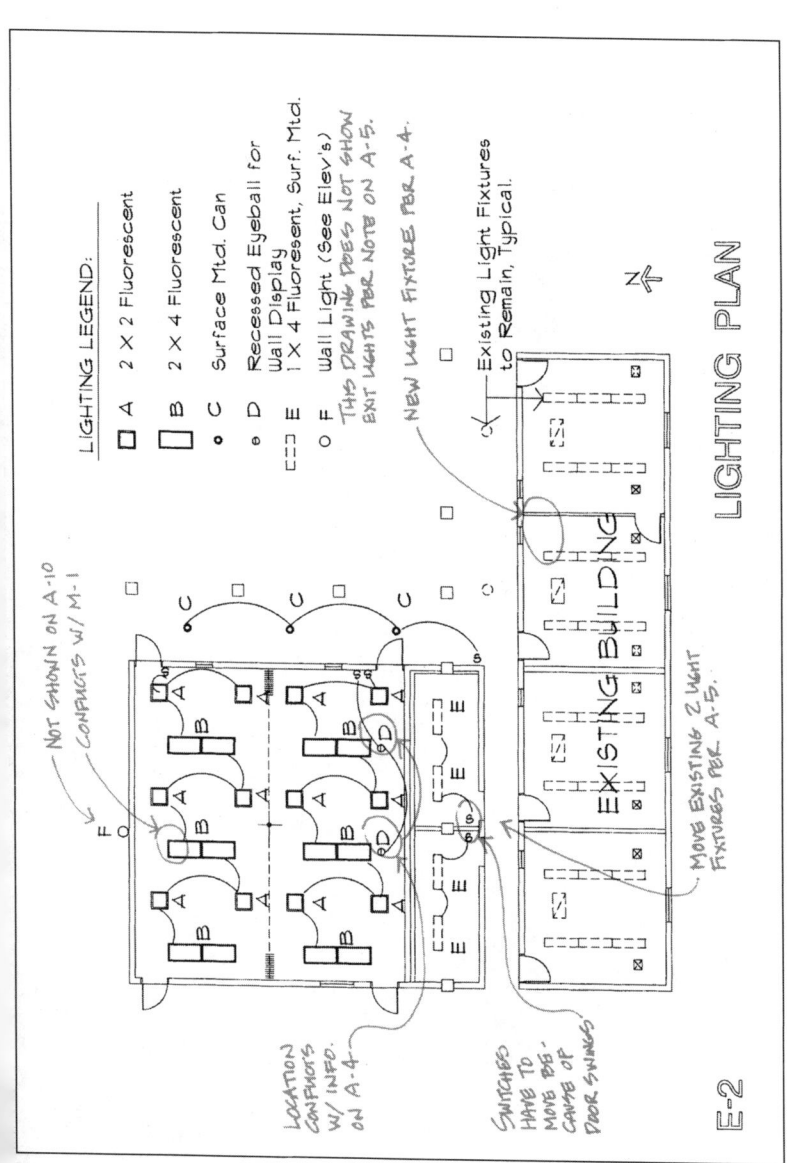

LIGHTING LEGEND:

☐ A   2 X 2 Fluorescent

▭ B   2 X 4 Fluorescent

○ C   Surface Mtd. Can

⊙ D   Recessed Eyeball for
       Wall Display

▭ E   1 X 4 Fluorescent, Surf. Mtd.

○ F   Wall Light (See Elev's)

THIS DRAWING DOES NOT SHOW
EXIT LIGHTS PER NOTE ON A-5.

NEW LIGHT FIXTURE PER A-4.

⊠ — Existing Light Fixtures
     to Remain, Typical.

NOT SHOWN ON A-10
CONFLICTS W/ M-1

LOCATION
CONFLICTS
W/ INFO.
ON A-4

SWITCHES
HAVE TO
MOVE BE-
CAUSE OF
DOOR SWINGS

MOVE EXISTING 2 LIGHT
FIXTURES PER. A-5.

EXISTING BUILDING

N

E-2   LIGHTING PLAN

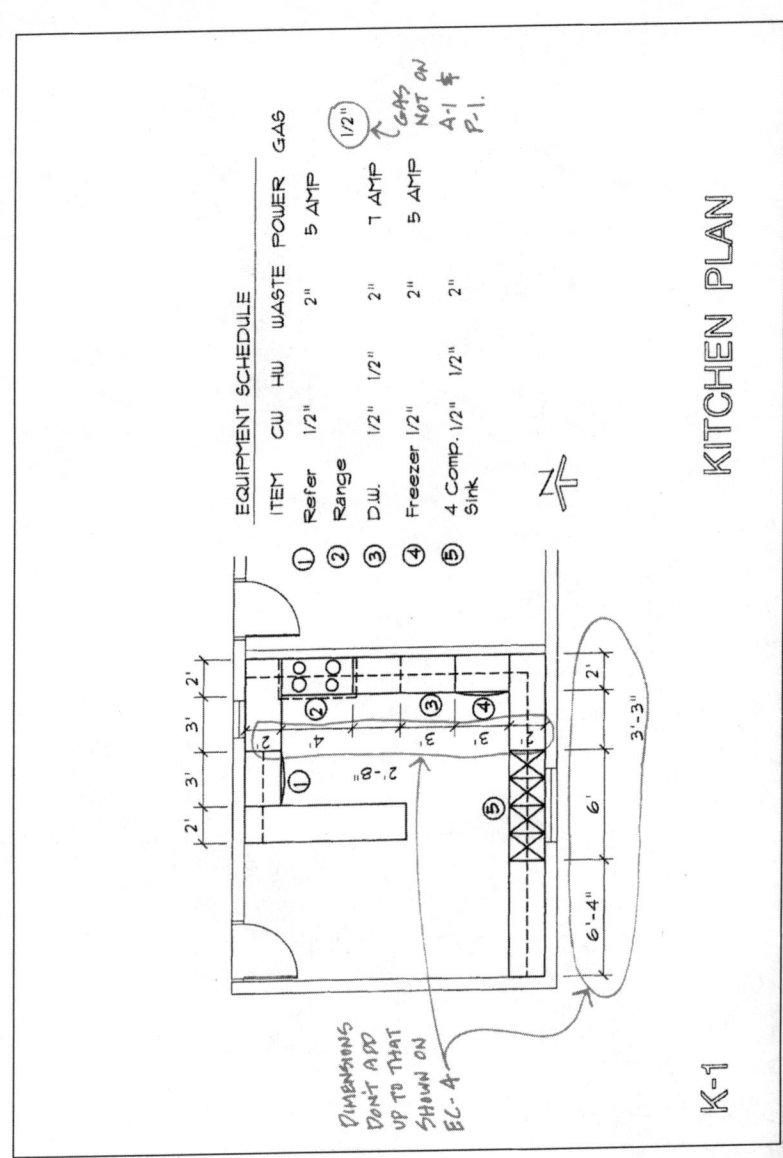

EQUIPMENT SCHEDULE

ITEM		CW	HW	WASTE	POWER	GAS
①	Refer	1/2"		2"	5 AMP	
②	Range					
③	D.W.	1/2"	1/2"	2"	7 AMP	
④	Freezer	1/2"		2"	5 AMP	
⑤	4 Comp. Sink	1/2"	1/2"	2"		

1/2"

GAS NOT ON A-1 & P-1.

KITCHEN PLAN

DIMENSIONS DON'T ADD UP TO THAT SHOWN ON EL-4

K-1

MULTIPURPOSE ROOM
ADDITION SPECIFICATIONS
TABLE OF CONTENTS

Exercise   _149_

DIVISION 5—METALS

____ 05100 STRUCTURAL METALS

____ 05500 MISC. METALS

DIVISION 6—WOOD AND PLASTICS

____ 06100 ROUGH CARPENTRY

____ 06200 FINISH CARPENTRY

____ 06400 ARCHITECTURAL WOODWORK

____ 06600 PLASTIC FABRICATIONS

DIVISION 7—THERMAL AND MOISTURE PROTECTION

____ 07500 MEMBRANE ROOFING ← ____ 07200 THERMAL PROTECTION (INSULATION) missing Per A-9 & 12

____ 07600 FLASHING AND SHEET METAL

____ 07900 JOINT SEALERS ← ____ 07800 ROOF ACCESSORIES (ROOF HATCH) missing Per A-7

DIVISION 8—DOORS AND WINDOWS

____ 08050 BASIC DOOR AND WINDOW MATERIALS AND METHODS

____ 08100 METAL DOORS AND FRAMES

____ 08500 WINDOWS ← ____ 08200 WOOD DOORS Per Dr. Schedule on A-8

____ 08700 HARDWARE

____ 08800 GLAZING

DIVISION 9—FINISHES

____ 09100 METAL SUPPORT ASSEMBLIES

____ 09200 PLASTER AND GYPSUM BOARD

____ 09300 TILE

____ 09400 TERRAZZO ← where is this on this Job?

____ 09500 CEILINGS

____ 09600 RESILIENT FLOORING

____ CARPET

____ 09900 PAINTING

DIVISION 10—SPECIALTIES

____ 10150 TOILET COMPARTMENTS

____ 10800 TOILET ACCESSORIES

DIVISION 11—EQUIPMENT

____ 11400 FOOD SERVICE EQUIPMENT

DIVISION 12—FURNISHINGS

____ 12100 ART

____ 12400 FURNISHINGS AND ACCESSORIES

____ 12500 FURNITURE

____ 12600 MULTIPLE SEATING

DIVISION 13—SPECIAL CONSTRUCTION

NOT USED

DIVISION 14—CONVEYING SYSTEMS

NOT USED

DIVISION 15—MECHANICAL

____ 15050 BASIC MECHANICAL MATERIALS AND METHODS

____ 15400 PLUMBING FIXTURES AND EQUIPMENT

____ 15700 HEATING, VENTILATING, AND AIR CONDITIONING

____ 15950 TESTING, ADJUSTING, AND BALANCING

DIVISION 16—ELECTRICAL

____ 16050 BASIC ELECTRICAL MATERIALS AND METHODS

____ 16200 ELECTRICAL POWER

____ 16500 LIGHTING

Exercise

Appendix A

Specifications
1995 C.S.I. Format*

INTRODUCTORY INFORMATION
- ____ 00001 PROJECT TITLE PAGE
- ____ 00005 CERTIFICATIONS PAGE
- ____ 00007 SEALS PAGE
- ____ 00010 TABLE OF CONTENTS
- ____ 00015 LIST OF DRAWINGS
- ____ 00020 LIST OF SCHEDULES

BIDDING REQUIREMENTS
- ____ 00100 BID SOLICITATION
- ____ 00200 INSTRUCTIONS TO BIDDERS
  - ____ 210 Supplementary Instructions to Bidders
  - ____ 220 Bid Scopes
  - ____ 250 Pre-Bid Meeting
- ____ 00300 INFORMATION AVAILABLE TO BIDDERS
  - ____ 310 Preliminary Schedules
  - ____ 320 Geotechnical Data
  - ____ 330 Existing Conditions
  - ____ 340 Environmental Assessment Information

*Reprinted by permission of The Construction Specifications Institute (CSI)

_____ 140   Work Restrictions
_____ 180   Project Utility Sources
_____ 01200   PRICE AND PAYMENT PROCEDURES
_____ 210   Allowances
_____ 230   Alternates
_____ 240   Value Analysis
_____ 250   Contract Modification Procedures
_____ 270   Unit Prices
_____ 290   Payment Procedures
_____ 01300   ADMINISTRATIVE REQUIREMENTS
_____ 310   Project Management and Coordination
_____ 320   Construction Progress Documentation
_____ 330   Submittal Procedures
_____ 350   Special Procedures
_____ 01400   QUALITY REQUIREMENTS
_____ 410   Regulatory Requirements
_____ 420   References
_____ 430   Quality Assurance
_____ 450   Quality Control
_____ 01500   TEMPORARY FACILITIES AND CONTROLS
_____ 510   Temporary Utilities
_____ 520   Construction Facilities
_____ 530   Temporary Construction
_____ 540   Construction Aids
_____ 550   Vehicular Access and Parking
_____ 560   Temporary Barriers and Enclosures
_____ 570   Temporary Controls
_____ 580   Project Identification
_____ 01600   PROJECT REQUIREMENTS
_____ 610   Basic Product Requirements
_____ 620   Product Options
_____ 630   Product Substitution Procedures
_____ 640   Owner-Furnished Products
_____ 650   Product Delivery Requirements
_____ 660   Product Storage and Handling
            Requirements
_____ 01700   EXECUTION REQUIREMENTS
_____ 710   Examination
_____ 720   Preparation

Specifications   _155_

	350	Concrete Finishing
	360	Concrete Finishes
	370	Specially Placed Concrete
	380	Post-Tensioned Concrete
	390	Concrete Curing

____ 03400 PRECAST CONCRETE

	410	Plant-Precast Structural Concrete
	420	Plant-Precast Structural Post-Tensioned Concrete
	430	Site-Precast Structural Concrete
	450	Plant-Precast Architectural Concrete
	460	Site-Precast Architectural Concrete
	470	Tilt-Up Precast Concrete
	480	Precast Concrete Specialties
	490	Glass-Fiber-Reinforced Precast Concrete

____ 03500 CEMENTITIOUS DECKS AND UNDERLAYMENT

	510	Cementitious Roof Deck
	520	Lightweight Concrete Roof Insulation
	530	Concrete Topping
	540	Cementitous Underlayment

____ 03600 GROUTS

____ 03700 MASS CONCRETE

____ 03900 CONCRETE RESTORATION AND CLEANING

	910	Concrete Cleaning
	920	Concrete Resurfacing
	930	Concrete Rehabilitation

DIVISION 4—MASONRY

____ 04050 BASIC MASONRY MATERIALS AND METHODS

	060	Masonry Mortar
	070	Masonry Grout
	080	Masonry Anchorage and Reinforcement
	090	Masonry Accessories

____ 04200 MASONRY UNITS

	210	Clay Masonry Units
	220	Concrete Masonry Units
	230	Calcium Silicate Unit Masonry
	270	Glass Masonry Units
	290	Adobe Masonry Units

____ 150 Wire Rope Assemblies
____ 160 Metal Framing Systems
____ 05200 METAL JOISTS
    ____ 210 Steel Joists
    ____ 250 Aluminum Joists
    ____ 260 Composite Joist Assemblies
____ 05300 METAL DECK
    ____ 310 Steel Deck
    ____ 320 Raceway Deck Systems
    ____ 330 Aluminum Deck
    ____ 340 Acoustical Metal Deck
____ 05400 COLD-FORMED METAL FRAMING
    ____ 410 Load-Bearing Metal Studs
    ____ 420 Cold-Formed Metal Joists
    ____ 430 Slotted Channel Framing
    ____ 450 Metal Support
____ 05500 METAL FABRICATIONS
    ____ 510 Metal Stairs and Ladders
    ____ 520 Handrails and Railings
    ____ 530 Gratings
    ____ 540 Floor Plates
    ____ 550 Stair Treads and Nosings
    ____ 560 Metal Castings
    ____ 580 Formed Metal Fabrications
____ 05600 HYDRAULIC FABRICATIONS
____ 05650 RAILROAD TRACK AND ACCESSORIES
____ 05700 ORNAMENTAL METAL
    ____ 710 Ornamental Stairs
    ____ 715 Fabricated Spiral Stairs
    ____ 720 Ornamental Handrails and Railings
    ____ 725 Ornamental Metal Castings
    ____ 730 Ornamental Formed Metal
    ____ 740 Ornamental Forged Metal
____ 05800 EXPANSION CONTROL
    ____ 810 Expansion Joint Cover Assemblies
    ____ 820 Slide Bearings
    ____ 830 Bridge Expansion Joint Assemblies
____ 05900 METAL RESTORATION AND CLEANING

DIVISION 6—WOOD AND PLASTICS

_____ 06050 BASIC WOOD AND PLASTIC MATERIALS AND METHODS

- _____ 060 Wood Materials
- _____ 065 Plastic Materials
- _____ 070 Wood Treatment
- _____ 080 Factory-Applied Wood Coatings
- _____ 090 Wood and Plastic Fastenings

_____ 06100 ROUGH CARPENTRY

- _____ 110 Wood Framing
- _____ 120 Structural Panels
- _____ 130 Heavy Timber Construction
- _____ 140 Treated Wood Foundations
- _____ 150 Wood Decking
- _____ 160 Sheating
- _____ 170 Prefabricated Structural Wood
- _____ 180 Glued-Laminated Construction

_____ 06200 FINISH CARPENTRY

- _____ 220 Millwork
- _____ 250 Prefinished Paneling
- _____ 260 Board Paneling
- _____ 270 Closet and Utility Wood Shelving

_____ 06400 ARCHITECTURAL WOODWORK

- _____ 410 Custom Cabinets
- _____ 415 Countertops
- _____ 420 Paneling
- _____ 430 Wood Stairs and Railings
- _____ 440 Wood Ornaments
- _____ 445 Simulated Wood Ornaments
- _____ 450 Standing and Running Trim
- _____ 455 Simulated Wood Trim
- _____ 460 Wood Frames
- _____ 470 Screens, Blinds, and Shutters

_____ 06500 STRUCTURAL PLASTICS

- _____ 510 Structural Plastic Shapes and Plates
- _____ 520 Plastic Structural Assemblies

_____ 06600 PLASTIC FABRICATIONS

	06900	WOOD AND PLASTIC RESTORATION AND CLEANING
		____ 910 Wood Restoration and Cleaning
		____ 920 Plastic Restoration and Cleaning

DIVISION 7—THERMAL AND MOISTURE PROTECTION

____ 07050 BASIC THERMAL AND MOISTURE PROTECTION MATERIALS AND METHODS

____ 07100 DAMPPROOFING AND WATERPROOFING
- ____ 110 Dampproofing
- ____ 120 Built-Up Bituminous Waterproofing
- ____ 130 Sheet Waterproofing
- ____ 140 Fluid-Applied Waterproofing
- ____ 150 Sheet Metal Waterproofing
- ____ 160 Cementitious and Reactive Waterproofing
- ____ 170 Bentonite Waterproofing
- ____ 180 Traffic Coatings
- ____ 190 Water Repellents

____ 07200 THERMAL PROTECTION
- ____ 210 Building Insulation
- ____ 220 Roof and Deck Insulation
- ____ 240 Exterior Insulation and Finish Systems (EIFS)
- ____ 260 Vapor Retarders
- ____ 270 Air Barriers

____ 07300 SHINGLES, ROOF TILES AND ROOF COVERINGS
- ____ 310 Shingles
- ____ 320 Roof Tiles
- ____ 330 Roof Coverings

____ 07400 ROOFING AND SIDING PANELS
- ____ 410 Metal Roof and Wall Panels
- ____ 420 Plastic Roof and Wall Panels
- ____ 430 Composite Panels
- ____ 440 Faced Panels
- ____ 450 Fiber-Reinforced Cementitous Panels
- ____ 460 Siding
- ____ 470 Wood Roof and Wall Panels
- ____ 480 Exterior Wall Assemblies

	07500		MEMBRANE ROOFING
____	07500		MEMBRANE ROOFING
		____ 510	Built-Up Roofing
		____ 520	Cold-Applied Bituminous Roofing
		____ 530	Elastomeric Membrane Roofing (CPE, CSPE, CPA, EDPM, NBP, PIB)
		____ 540	Thermoplastic Membrane Roofing (EIP, PVC, TPA)
		____ 550	Modified Bituminous Membrane Roofing
		____ 560	Fluid-Applied Roofing
		____ 570	Coated Foamed Roofing
		____ 580	Roll Roofing
		____ 590	Roof Maintenance and Repairs
____	07600		FLASHING AND SHEET METAL
		____ 610	Sheet Metal Roofing
		____ 620	Sheet Metal Flashing and Trim
		____ 630	Sheet Metal Roofing Specialties
		____ 650	Flexible Flashing
____	07700		ROOF SPECIALTIES AND ACCESSORIES
		____ 710	Manufactured Roof Specialties
		____ 720	Roof Accessories
		____ 730	Roof Pavers
____	07800		FIRE AND SMOKE PROTECTION
		____ 810	Applied Fireproofing
		____ 820	Board Fireproofing
		____ 840	Firestopping
		____ 860	Smoke Seals
		____ 870	Smoke Containment Barriers
____	07900		JOINT SEALERS
		____ 910	Preformed Joint Seals
		____ 920	Joint Sealants

DIVISION 8—DOORS AND WINDOWS

____	08050		BASIC DOOR AND WINDOW MATERIALS AND METHODS
____	08100		METAL DOORS AND FRAMES
		____ 110	Steel Doors and Frames
		____ 120	Aluminum Doors and Frames
		____ 130	Stainless Steel Doors and Frames
		____ 140	Bronze Doors and Frames

____	150	Preassembled Metal Doors and Frames
____	160	Sliding Metal Doors and Grilles
____	180	Metal Screen and Storm Doors
____	190	Metal Door Restoration

____ 08200 WOOD AND PLASTIC DOORS

____	210	Wood Doors
____	220	Plastic Doors
____	250	Preassembled Wood and Plastic Doors and Frame Units
____	260	Sliding Wood and Plastic Doors
____	280	Wood and Plastic Storm and Screen Doors
____	260	Wood and Plastic Doors Restoration

____ 08300 SPECIALTY DOORS

____	310	Access Doors and Panels
____	320	Detention Doors and Frames
____	330	Coiling Doors and Grilles
____	340	Special Function Doors
____	350	Folding Doors and Grilles
____	360	Overhead Doors
____	370	Vertical Lift Doors
____	380	Traffic Doors
____	390	Pressure-Resistant Doors

____ 08400 ENTRANCES AND STOREFRONTS

____	410	Metal-Framed Storefronts
____	450	All-Glass Entrances and Storefronts
____	460	Automatic Entrance Doors
____	470	Revolving Entrance Doors
____	480	Balanced Entrance Doors
____	490	Sliding Storefronts

____ 08500 WINDOWS

____	510	Steel Windows
____	520	Aluminum Windows
____	530	Stainless Steel Windows
____	540	Bronze Windows
____	550	Wood Windows
____	560	Plastic Windows
____	570	Composite Windows
____	580	Special Function Windows
____	590	Window Restoration and Replacement

_____ 08600 SKYLIGHTS
         _____ 610 Roof Windows
         _____ 620 Unit Skylights
         _____ 630 Metal-Framed Skylights

_____ 08700 HARDWARE
         _____ 710 Door Hardware
         _____ 720 Weatherstripping and Seals
         _____ 740 Electro-Mechanical Hardware
         _____ 750 Window Hardware
         _____ 770 Door and Window Accessories
         _____ 780 Special Function Hardware
         _____ 790 Hardware Restoration

_____ 08800 GLAZING
         _____ 810 Glass
         _____ 830 Mirrors
         _____ 840 Plastic Glazing
         _____ 850 Glazing Accessories
         _____ 890 Glazing Restoration

_____ 08900 GLAZED CURTAIN WALL
         _____ 910 Metal Framed Curtain Wall
         _____ 950 Translucent Wall and Roof Assemblies
         _____ 960 Sloped Glazing Assemblies
         _____ 970 Structural Glass Curtain Wall
         _____ 990 Glazed Curtain Wall Restoration

DIVISION 9—FINISHES

_____ 09050 BASIC FINISH MATERIALS AND METHODS

_____ 09100 METAL SUPPORT ASSEMBLIES
         _____ 110 Non-Load-Bearing Wall Framing
         _____ 120 Ceiling Suspension
         _____ 130 Acoustical Suspension
         _____ 190 Metal Frame Restoration

_____ 09200 PLASTER AND GYPSUM BOARD
         _____ 205 Furring and Lathing
         _____ 210 Gypsum Plaster
         _____ 220 Portland Cement Plaster
         _____ 230 Plaster Fabrications
         _____ 250 Gypsum Board
         _____ 260 Gypsum Board Assemblies

____ 270 Gypsum Board Accessories

____ 280 Plaster Restoration

____ 09300 TILE

    ____ 305 Tile Setting Materials and Accessories

    ____ 310 Ceramic Tile

    ____ 330 Quarry Tile

    ____ 340 Paver Tile

    ____ 350 Glass Mosaics

    ____ 360 Plastic Tile

    ____ 370 Metal Tile

    ____ 380 Cut Natural Stone Tile

    ____ 390 Tile Restoration

____ 09400 TERRAZZO

    ____ 410 Portland Cement Terrazzo

    ____ 420 Precast Terrazzo

    ____ 430 Conductive Terrazzo

    ____ 440 Plastic Matrix Terrazzo

    ____ 490 Terrazzo Restoration

____ 09500 CEILINGS

    ____ 510 Acoustical Ceilings

    ____ 545 Specialty Ceilings

    ____ 550 Mirror Panel Ceilings

    ____ 560 Textured Ceilings

    ____ 570 Linear Wood Ceilings

    ____ 580 Suspended Decorated Grids

    ____ 590 Ceiling Assembly Restoration

____ 09600 FLOORING

    ____ 610 Floor Treatment

    ____ 620 Specialty Flooring

    ____ 630 Masonry Flooring

    ____ 640 Wood Flooring

    ____ 650 Resilient Flooring

    ____ 660 Static Control Flooring

    ____ 670 Fluid-Applied Flooring

    ____ 680 Carpet

    ____ 690 Flooring Restoration

____ 09700 WALL FINISHES

    ____ 710 Acoustical Wall Treatment

    ____ 720 Wall Covering

_____ 730 Wall Carpet
_____ 740 Flexible Wood Sheets
_____ 750 Stone Facing
_____ 760 Plastic Blocks
_____ 770 Special Wall Surfaces
_____ 790 Wall Finish Restoration

_____ 09800 ACOUSTICAL TREATMENT
_____ 810 Acoustical Space Units
_____ 820 Acoustical Insulation and Sealants
_____ 830 Acoustical Barriers
_____ 840 Acoustical Wall Treatment

_____ 09900 PAINTS AND COATINGS
_____ 910 Paints
_____ 930 Stains and Transparent Finishes
_____ 940 Decorative Finishes
_____ 960 High-Performance Coatings
_____ 970 Coatings for Steel
_____ 980 Coatings for Concrete and Masonry
_____ 990 Paint Restoration

DIVISION 10—SPECIALTIES

_____ 10100 VISUAL DISPLAY BOARDS
_____ 110 Chalkboards
_____ 115 Markerboards
_____ 120 Tackboards and Visual Aid Boards
_____ 130 Operable Board Units
_____ 140 Display Track Assemblies
_____ 145 Visual Aid Board Units

_____ 10150 COMPARTMENTS AND CUBICLES
_____ 160 Metal Toilet Compartments
_____ 165 Plastic Laminate Toilet Compartments
_____ 170 Plastic Toilet Compartments
_____ 175 Particleboard Toilet Compartments
_____ 180 Stone Toilet Compartments
_____ 185 Shower and Dressing Compartments
_____ 190 Cubicles

_____ 10200 LOUVERS AND VENTS
_____ 210 Wall Louvers
_____ 220 Louvered Equipment Enclosures

Specifications

____ 10750 TELEPHONE SPECIALTIES

____ 10800 TOILET, BATH, AND LAUNDRY ACCESSORIES

        ____ 810 Toilet Accessories

        ____ 820 Bath Accessories

        ____ 830 Laundry Accessories

____ 10880 SCALES

____ 10900 WARDROBE AND CLOSET SPECIALTIES

DIVISION 11—EQUIPMENT

____ 11010 MAINTENANCE EQUIPMENT

____ 11020 SECURITY AND VAULT EQUIPMENT

____ 11030 TELLER AND SERVICE EQUIPMENT

____ 11040 ECCLESIASTICAL EQUIPMENT

____ 11050 LIBRARY EQUIPMENT

____ 11060 THEATER AND STAGE EQUIPMENT

____ 11070 INSTRUMENTAL EQUIPMENT

____ 11080 REGISTRATION EQUIPMENT

____ 11090 CHECKROOM EQUIPMENT

____ 11100 MERCANTILE EQUIPMENT

____ 11110 COMMERCIAL LAUNDRY AND DRY CLEANING EQUIPMENT

____ 11120 VENDING EQUIPMENT

____ 11130 AUDIO-VISUAL EQUIPMENT

____ 11140 VEHICLE SERVICE EQUIPMENT

____ 11150 PARKING CONTROL EQUIPMENT

____ 11160 LOADING DOCK EQUIPMENT

____ 11170 SOLID WASTE HANDLING EQUIPMENT

____ 11190 DETENTION EQUIPMENT

____ 11200 WATER SUPPLY AND TREATMENT EQUIPMENT

        ____ 210 Supply and Treatment Pumps

        ____ 220 Mixers and Flocculators

        ____ 225 Clarifiers

        ____ 230 Water Aeration Equipment

        ____ 240 Chemical Feed equipment

        ____ 250 Water Softening Equipment

        ____ 260 Disinfectant Feed Equipment

        ____ 270 Fluoridation Equipment

____ 11280 HYDRAULIC GATES AND VALVES
    ____ 285 Hydraulic Gates
    ____ 285 Hydraulic Valves

____ 11300 FLUID WASTE TREATMENT AND DISPOSAL EQUIPMENT
    ____ 310 Sewage and Sludge Pumps
    ____ 320 Grit Collecting Equipment
    ____ 330 Screening and Grinding Equipment
    ____ 335 Sedimentation Tank Equipment
    ____ 340 Scum Removal Equipment
    ____ 345 Chemical Equipment
    ____ 350 Sludge Handling and Treatment Equipment
    ____ 360 Filter Press Equipment
    ____ 365 Tracking Filter Equipment
    ____ 370 Compressors
    ____ 375 Aeration Equipment
    ____ 380 Sludge Digestion Equipment
    ____ 385 Digester Mixing Equipment
    ____ 390 Package Sewage Treatment Plants

____ 11400 FOOD SERVICE EQUIPMENT
    ____ 405 Food Storage Equipment
    ____ 410 Food Preparation Equipment
    ____ 415 Food Delivery Carts and Conveyors
    ____ 420 Food Cooking Equipment
    ____ 425 Hood and Ventilation Equipment
    ____ 430 Food Dispensing Equipment
    ____ 435 Ice Machines
    ____ 440 Cleaning and Disposal Equipment

____ 11450 RESIDENTIAL EQUIPMENT
____ 11460 UNIT KITCHENS
____ 11470 DARKROOM EQUIPMENT
____ 11480 ATHLETIC, RECREATIONAL, AND THERAPEUTIC EQUIPMENT
____ 11500 INDUSTRIAL AND PROCESS EQUIPMENT
____ 11600 LABORATORY EQUIPMENT
____ 11650 PLANETARIUM EQUIPMENT
____ 11660 OBSERVATORY EQUIPMENT
____ 11680 OFFICE EQUIPMENT

____ 11700 MEDICAL EQUIPMENT
        ____ 710 Medical Sterilizing Equipment
        ____ 720 Examination and Treatment Equipment
        ____ 730 Patient Care Equipment
        ____ 740 Dental Equipment
        ____ 750 Optical Equipment
        ____ 760 Operating Room Equipment
        ____ 770 Radiology Equipment
____ 11780 MORTUARY EQUIPMENT
____ 11850 NAVIGATION EQUIPMENT
____ 11870 AGRICULTURAL EQUIPMENT
____ 11900 EXHIBIT EQUIPMENT

DIVISION 12—FURNISHINGS

____ 12050 FABRICS
____ 12100 ART
        ____ 110 Murals
        ____ 120 Wall Decorations
        ____ 140 Sculptures
        ____ 170 Art Glass
        ____ 190 Ecclesiastical Art
____ 12300 MANUFACTURED CASEWORK
        ____ 310 Manufactured Metal Casework
        ____ 320 Manufactured Wood Casework
        ____ 350 Specialty Casework
____ 12400 FURNISHINGS AND ACCESSORIES
        ____ 410 Office Accessories
        ____ 420 Table Accessories
        ____ 430 Portable lamps
        ____ 440 Bath Furnishings
        ____ 450 Bedroom Furnishings
        ____ 460 Furnishing Accessories
        ____ 480 Rugs and Mats
        ____ 490 Window Treatments
____ 12500 FURNITURE
        ____ 510 Office Furniture
        ____ 520 Seating

	540	Hospitality Furniture
	560	Institutional Furniture
	580	Residential Furniture

____ 12600 MULTIPLE SEATING
	610	Fixed Audience Seating
	620	Portable Audience Seating
	630	Stadium and Arena Seating
	640	Booths and Tables
	650	Multiple-Use Fixed Seating
	660	Telescoping Stands
	670	Pews and Benches
	680	Seat and Table Assemblies

____ 12700 SYSTEMS FURNITURE
	710	Panel-Hung Component System Furniture
	720	Free-Standing Component System Furniture
	730	Beam System Furniture
	740	Desk System Furniture

____ 12800 INTERIOR PLANTS AND PLANTERS
	810	Interior Live Plants
	820	Interior Artificial Plants
	830	Interior Planters
	840	Interior Landscape Accessories
	850	Interior Plant Maintenance

____ 12900 FURNISHINGS RESTORATION AND REPAIR

DIVISION 13—SPECIAL CONSTRUCTION

____ 13010 AIR-SUPPORTED STRUCTURES

____ 13020 BUILDING MODULES

____ 13030 SPECIAL PURPOSE ROOMS

____ 13080 SOUND, VIBRATION AND SEISMIC CONTROL

____ 13090 RADIATION PROTECTION

____ 13100 LIGHTNING PROTECTION

____ 13110 CATHODIC PROTECTION

____ 13120 PRE-ENGINEERED STRUCTURES

____ 13150 SWIMMING POOLS

____ 13160 AQUARIUMS

____ 13165 AQUATIC PARK FACILITIES

____ 13800 BUILDING AUTOMATION AND CONTROL

____ 13850 DETECTION AND ALARM

____ 13900 FIRE SUPPRESSION

      ____ 910 Fire Protection Basic Materials and Methods

      ____ 920 Fire Pumps

      ____ 930 Wet-Pipe Fire Suppression Sprinklers

      ____ 935 Dry-Pipe Fire Suppression Sprinklers

      ____ 940 Pre-Action Fire Suppression Sprinklers

      ____ 945 Combination Dry-Pipe and Pre-Action Fire Suppression Sprinklers

      ____ 950 Deluge Fire Suppression Sprinklers

      ____ 955 Foam Fire Extinguishing

      ____ 960 Carbon Dioxide Fire Extinguishing

      ____ 965 Alternative Fire Extinguishing Systems

      ____ 970 Dry Chemical Fire Extinguishing

      ____ 975 Standpipes and Hoses

DIVISION 14—CONVEYING SYSTEMS

____ 14100 DUMBWAITERS

      ____ 110 Manual Dumbwaiters

      ____ 120 Electric Dumbwaiters

      ____ 140 Hydraulic Dumbwaiters

____ 14200 ELEVATORS

      ____ 210 Electric Traction Elevators

      ____ 240 Hydraulic Elevators

      ____ 270 Custom Elevators Cabs

      ____ 280 Elevator Equipment and Controls

      ____ 290 Elevator Renovation

____ 14300 ESCALATORS AND MOVING WALKS

____ 14400 LIFTS

      ____ 410 People Lifts

      ____ 420 Wheelchair Lifts

      ____ 430 Platform Lifts

      ____ 440 People Lifts

      ____ 450 Vehicle Lifts

____ 14500 MATERIAL HANDLING

      ____ 510 Material Transport

      ____ 530 Postal Conveying

      ____ 540 Baggage Conveying and Dispensing

_____ 130 Pumps
_____ 140 Domestic Water Piping
_____ 150 Sanitary Waste and Vent Piping
_____ 160 Storm Drainage Piping
_____ 170 Swimming Pool and Fountain Piping
_____ 180 Heating and Cooling Piping
_____ 190 Fuel Piping
_____ 15200 PROCESS PIPING
_____ 210 Process Air and Gas Piping
_____ 220 Process Water and Waste Piping
_____ 230 Industrial Process Piping
_____ 15300 FIRE PROTECTION
_____ 15400 PLUMBING FIXTURES AND EQUIPMENT
_____ 410 Plumbing Fixtures
_____ 440 Plumbing Pumps
_____ 450 Potable Water Storage Tanks
_____ 460 Domestic Water Conditioning Equipment
_____ 470 Domestic Water Filtrating Equipment
_____ 480 Domestic Water Heaters
_____ 490 Pool and Fountain Equipment
_____ 15500 HEAT-GENERATION EQUIPMENT
_____ 510 Heating Boilers and Accessories
_____ 520 Feedwater Equipment
_____ 530 Furnaces
_____ 540 Fuel-Fired Heaters
_____ 550 Breechings, Chimneys, and Stacks
_____ 15600 REFRIGERATION EQUIPMENT
_____ 610 Refrigeration Compressors
_____ 620 Packaged Water Chillers
_____ 630 Refrigerant Monitoring Systems
_____ 640 Packaged Cooling Towers
_____ 650 Field-Erected Cooling Towers
_____ 660 Liquid Coolers and Evaporative Condensers
_____ 670 Refrigerant Condensing Units
_____ 15700 HEATING, VENTILATING, AND AIR CONDITIONING EQUIPMENT
_____ 710 Heat Exchanger
_____ 720 Air Handling Units
_____ 730 Unitary Air Conditioning Equipment
_____ 740 Heat Pumps

About the Author

John Patten ("Pat") Guthrie, AIA, is a Principal of John Pat Guthrie Architects, Inc., of Scottsdale, Arizona. A licensed architect in 13 states, he heads a broad-based practice that includes commercial, residential, industrial, medical, and religious facilities and that also specializes in passive solar energy design. Mr. Guthrie is author of the best-selling *Architect's Portable Handbook*, published by McGraw-Hill and now in its second edition.